Notorious San Francisco:

True Tales of Crime, Passion and Murder

by Paul Drexler

"This is a work of nonfiction. No names have been changed, no characters invented, no events fabricated."

Notorious San Francisco:

True Tales of Crime, Passion and Murder

by Paul Drexler

ISBN: 978-1-7923-6830-1

Copyright and Published June 2021

2nd Edition

by AD Publishing

Acknowledgements

My destination as a writer has always been a published book. I'd like to thank the many people who helped me to complete this long journey.

Thanks to the San Francisco Examiner who gave me the space and the deadlines to develop these stories. To the late R.J. Parker, my publisher who said "yes" quickly, when others said "no" in slow motion.

To the San Francisco History Association, the San Francisco Public Library, the Mechanics Library, California State Archives, San Quentin Museum librarian Jeff Craemer, Ken Moses, who established the SFPD CSI unit, the Writers Grotto, the late Ricky Jay, Lezlie Micheletti, Lloyd Samsell's granddaughter, and the retired SFPD, who gave their time and support.

To my Uncle Jack's 1951 Buick, whose role in a New Jersey gangland murder sparked my interest in crime.

To my daughters, Lily and Michelle Drexler, my brother, Hank Drexler, and the memory of my parents, Julien and Shirley Drexler.

Thanks to Rob Kavet, who designed the book's cover.

Special thanks to my editor Bill Snyder, and my sagacious wife, Julie Marsh, for her astute suggestions and assistance.

I dedicate this book to my friend, mentor, and crime history maven, the late Kevin Mullen, Retired Deputy Police Chief, SFPD.

PRAISE FOR THE BOOK

"Paul Drexler takes us on a trip into San Francisco's underworld that's entertaining, fascinating, and insightful. From 'jazzmania' to 'zodiology,' Notorious San Francisco provides a jaw-dropping glimpse into the city's criminal history." —

Meg Gardiner, author of UNSUB

"This book paints a broad strokes view of San Francisco's most infamous criminals, a fascinating lineup of desperadoes, con men (and women), thieves and murderers. It should be required reading of anyone seriously interested in the underground history of Baghdad By The Bay.

Plus — a bonus — it's simply a hell of a lot of fun to read!"

John Lescroat, *New York Times* bestselling author

"Crime Historian Paul Drexler takes the reader back to a time when San Francisco was a bustling port city with an impressive criminal underworld that you never knew about. Murders and scams litter the streets of San Francisco like last week's SF Weekly. Drexler names names and gives out addresses.

He writes about these long dead celebrity criminals without moralizing or glorifying their actions, but with a knowing grin."

David Kulczyk, author of Death in California

"You won't be disappointed by this book. Paul Drexler describes events in San Francisco and makes you feel as though you are there observing. The stories he weaves are true, though they sound as though they were created for a TV show. The characters are fascinating, and they are real!"

Steal this Book

Kirkus Review

A debut set of true crime essays explores San Francisco's dark side. Drexler wrote the column "Notorious Crooks" for the Sunday *San Francisco Examiner* from 2014 to 2018 and runs walking tours of the area's crime hot spots. In this work, he collects bizarre, seedy tales of notorious culprits and unsolved mysteries, covering a century from the 1870s through the 1980s.

The infamous characters surveyed include Juanita "Duchess" Spinelli, a "modern-day Fagin" who ran a crime school and was "the first woman to be executed in California"; obese "gambling czar" Elmer "Bones" Remmer; and Dorothy Ellingson, who in 1925 killed her mother for threatening to send her to reform school—her insanity plea failed. The press blamed cars and music for the 16-year-old's degeneracy, branding her a "Jazzmaniac." Drexler takes readers on a sprightly tour through the car thefts and holdups of the Terror Bandits, attempted murders, and more.

The stories of female criminals feel less familiar and thus tend to stand out, especially those of Inez Burns, an abortionist who performed as many as 30 procedures a week and was rumored to have had Rita Hayworth as a patient, and Sally Stanford, who ran a speak-easy and then a brothel. The disparity in how these two women fared says something about the shifting morality of the 20th century.

While Burns, whose services had formerly been considered a "necessary evil," was indicted in 1946, serving two years in prison and paying hundreds of thousand dollars in back taxes. Stanford went on to run for the Sausalito City Council (she won on her sixth attempt) and was later elected mayor. A longer, final section deftly focuses on the Zodiac Killer case, which Drexler (who has appeared on television as an expert on the crimes) calls "the most famous unsolved murder mystery of modern times."

The author makes good use of primary sources such as court transcripts, providing an appropriate level of detail that never seems gratuitous or overly sordid. Black-and-white photographs are provided for many of the historical figures discussed.

A lighthearted, informative take on rather grim events.

TABLE OF CONTENTS

Acknowledgements *5*

Dangerous Women 1
Jazzmania 2
The Duchess... 11
The Grandma from Hell....................................14
Isabella J. Martin, The Queen of Grudges 25

Serial Killers... 31
The Terror Bandits 33
    The Crimes... 33
    The Punishment 37
Earle Nelson: The Dark Strangler 41
The Buttermilk Bluebeard..................................51
The House on Billionaire Street........................ 59

Purveyors of Sin 69
Jerome Bassity: King of the Tenderloin........... 70
A Necessary Evil 75
Bones Remmer 80
Sally Stanford From Madam to Mayor............ 84

Con Artists... 89
The Confidence Queen 90
The Great Diamond Hoax 96
    The Hook.. 97
    The Payoff 99
    The Scam Revealed.................................. 100
The Man of 1000 Aliases................................ 104
The Father of Electrical Medicine 109

Masters of Escape 115
The Literate Larcenist 116
King of the Escape Artists 123
Manhunt: The Joe Tanko Story 127
The Yacht Bandits.. 133

Unsolved Mysteries.................................... **147**
    Was he Erdnase? 148
    The Preparedness Day Bombing..................... 154
    The Zodiac Killer 162
        The Crimes.................................. 163
    The Suspects 170
        My Father Was the Zodiac! 174

Nondenominational Zodiology................ **177**
    Zodiac Atheists 177
    The Radian Theory 180

Bonus Case: Killer Confectioner: The Sweet Gifts of Cordelia Botkin **185**

    About the Author.. *193*

Sources.. **195**

DANGEROUS WOMEN

Dangerous women fascinate us. Millions of people followed the murder trials of Casey Anthony and Jodi Arias. "Deadly Women," the popular ID Network show about women killers, is now in its 12th season. Oprah's channel, The Oxygen Network, is now an all true-crime channel, with programs such as "Martinis and Murder," "Celebrity Scandals" and "Social Media Crimes."

The women in this section are distinctive, and their crimes are most unusual. Sixteen-year-old Dorothy Ellingson's crime was, at the time, almost without precedent. Sadly, it has become commonplace today. Isabella Martin was the bane of Northern California's judicial system for ten years. Had the lawyers and judges known what she was really planning, they would have been absolutely terrified. Juanita "Duchess" Spinelli was a female Fagin who ran a deadly crime school in San Francisco and included her children as students. Iva Kroeger was a con woman whose harmless exterior disguised the deadly psychopath within.

Paul Drexler

Jazzmania

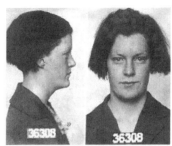

Dorothy Elllingson. Mugshot of a 16-year-old killer.
(California State archives, 1926)

In 1925, 16-year-old Dorothy Ellingson shot her mother, created a new disease, and inspired world literature.

Dorothy lived at 256 Third Avenue in San Francisco's Inner Richmond with her father, who was a tailor, her mother, and an older brother. She was a tall girl with flaming red hair and a temperament to match. "There is something in my heart that makes me hate rules and regular hours. I like to do things when I feel like doing them or I don't want to do them at all," said Dorothy, after her arrest. From the age of 14, Dorothy cut school during the day and snuck out to jazz clubs at night. Her ticket in was a fake ID showing her age as 19.

For months, her mother, Anna, tried to keep Dorothy home at night. Finally, on January 13, Anna threatened to send her daughter to reform school if she went out dancing that night. Furious, Dorothy found her brother's gun and shot her mother in the back.

Then she took $45, hurriedly packed a suitcase, went to the party, and danced the night away.

Her brother discovered the body later that day and called the police. The murder was splashed across the headlines the next day, and a huge girl hunt began. The case was a nationwide sensation. "Not in the history of California crime have I found a case where a daughter killed her mother," said District Attorney Matthew Brady. "I know of no case where a minor has been guilty of this crime."

"The Dorothy Ellingson case is the worst I've ever heard; more shocking by far than any of the 30,000 cases I handled," said Stella Miner, director of the Girls Security League of America. "I have studied girls who were thieves, moral degenerates and criminals of the lowest type," she said, "but this case is beyond my comprehension."

Miss Miner's recommendations for cases such as Dorothy's represented a 1920s attitude towards eugenics and child development. "At the first sign that she is delinquent or feeble-minded, the girl should be placed where she cannot get into more serious difficulties. Psychological examination should be given in grade school, and the child who is unmistakably a moron or degenerate should be placed in the colony of feeble-minded and kept there for life," wrote one "expert" at the time.

It was the heyday of Front-Page journalism and William Randolph Hearst's San Francisco Examiner, which had close ties to the police department, led the pack. The Examiner printed pages from Dorothy's diary, which revealed frequent trips to the New

Shanghai Café in Chinatown and her crowd of girlfriends and jazz musicians. "I went to Joe's party and met an amazing musician. He knows how to use all of his instruments," was one of the entries. Some of the entries were enigmatic, bordering on poetry. "Who done it you could know. I go. I go forever. I go. Have to go to poolroom. Gentlemen only. Forever in sincerity. God."

The press called her "the red-headed, bobbed-hair 'jazzmania' addict," soon shortened to "Jazzmaniac."

"Automobiles started me, and music finished me," claimed Dorothy. "I was always chasing that something which would bring me happiness and never seemed to find it," confessed Dorothy.

She was arrested the next day. At first, Dorothy blamed the killing on a man named Jimmy La Marr but soon confessed to the crime.

The Examiner scored another scoop, getting a three-part confession written by Dorothy Ellingson herself, entitled "Gun Wielder Bares Secret of Jazz Soul." Next to this article was one by star journalist Annie Laurie, entitled, "Dorothy Ellingson Egoist Who Thinks Only About Herself."

On the basis of Dorothy's confession, 17 musicians (aka "Sheiks" in 1920's slang) who worked at the New Shanghai Café were arrested on morals charges -- or perhaps as a way of reducing the risk of jazz infections. "We are going after the Sheiks who make the bright light district their rendezvous," declared Detective Captain Duncan Matheson. "If Dorothy Ellingson was led to murder by what she learned in public dance halls and cafes, we will find a way to clean up these places."

The case was an international sensation and dominated the news for months. F. Scott Fitzgerald followed the case closely from Paris, and it strongly influenced the first draft of his book, Tender is the Night. It was going to be a novel about expatriate life on the Riviera in which its hero, Francis Malarky, murders his mother. The book was tentatively titled "The Boy Who Killed his Mother."

There was no shortage of explanations for Dorothy's actions, starting with Dorothy herself. "Automobiles started me and music finished me," began her explanation, in a story titled "Mother Slayer Blames Her Plight to Auto Petting Parties, Lure of Music."

"She is the product of her environment," said University of California Psychologist Dr. Olga Bridgman. Reverend James Gordon blamed her situation on "The auto - the telephone - the movie - the novel - the café - the dance hall! The swirl, sex freedom, absence of control, irresponsibility!"

"Sound religious training should take the place of dance halls," said the Federation of Women's Clubs.

Sounding a contemporary note, Reverend Howard Blackney of the Howard Street Church inveighed against the practice of men going around armed and the tendency of Americans to have firearms in the homes.

Dorothy's actions were so unbelievable at the time that many believed they must have had an organic cause. Dr. Mary Halton, a leading endocrinologist, attributed Dorothy's actions to an overactive thyroid gland. Others argued that the problem was in Dorothy's mind. Stella Miner, director of the Girl's Security League, used Trumpish language when she characterized the shooting as the act of a "feeble-minded diseased moron."

"Psychological examinations should be given in all grades at school, and the child who is unmistakably a moron or a degenerate should be placed in a colony of feeble-minded people and kept there for life," Miner said.

The term "Jazzmania" was used to imply that popular music was responsible for the murder. The nation's Episcopal bishops held jazz-induced madness responsible for rising rates of divorce, suicide, and crime among young people. Jazz was described as a "virus infecting American society."

"Jazz goes back to the African jungle, and its effect is to make you ... want to go on all-fours and whisk your tail around a tree," asserted an Episcopal minister.

The first legal question was Dorothy's sanity, and a jury was impaneled to decide. Her defense attorney, Alexander Mooslin, said that prenatal influences from her mother helped drive Dorothy insane. "We will prove that one night her father was awakened by the clutch of his wife's hands around his throat; that she attempted to kill him as he slept and then fell in a hysterical fit on the floor." He said that Dorothy's mother and father separated about a year before Mrs. Ellingson's death.

Dr. Fred Clark, Superintendent of the State Hospital for the Insane, said that Dorothy suffered from "dementia praecox", the insanity of youth. Dr. Jau Ball agreed, testifying that Dorothy's rapid reactions to stimuli show that she acts without thinking.

The state's psychiatrists declared with equal certainty that Dorothy was legally sane, albeit disturbed. Dorothy loudly protested her defense's argument and declared that she was sane and wanted to go to trial. Her declarations were undercut by her courtroom actions: fainting and sobbing frequently, smashing a bottle of smelling salts, and throwing a glass of water at her attorneys.

The jury found her insane by a vote of 11 to 1, causing her to faint once more. She was then sent to Napa State Hospital. Newspaper editorials approved the decision. "It should be gratifying ...to know that Dorothy has been turned over to science instead of a prison." Her attorneys predicted that she would never be tried, and the case seemed to be over. But on May 20th, after five weeks of testing, nine Napa State psychiatrists unanimously proclaimed Dorothy sane, and a murder trial was scheduled.

On May 22nd, a new headline screamed from the newspapers, "Mystery Woman Involved in Jazz Girl Confession."

Dorothy had gone back to her original story in which she blamed the murder on Jimmy La Marr. According to her tale, Jimmy, a drug addict, came to call on her one morning. While she was getting ready, she heard Jimmy talking to her mother. All of a sudden, she heard a gunshot and entered the room, only to see her mother lying on the floor. Jimmy gave her $45, told her to hide out, and said not to mention him to anyone.

The next day a mysterious woman contacted her and "told me to say (in case I was arrested) that I committed the act, because nothing could be done with me, while if Jimmy were caught, I knew what that would mean."

Police and prosecutors scoffed at her story. "She was just entertaining the doctors at Napa with a good story," said Captain Matheson. He called La Marr a "mythical" person. The trial was scheduled for late June. During this time, Dorothy managed to keep in the news by having appendicitis and by converting to Catholicism.

Then, just before the trial, on June 19th, Prosecutor Harmon Skillen announced that Jimmy La Marr had been located. Skillen confidently added, "We have a bombshell ready to explode at the proper time at the trial. There is no use at touching a match to it and exploding it now." The bombshell turned out to be a dud. La Marr had nothing to do with the killing, said the police. The defense didn't call him, and he disappeared without ever being seen.

The prosecution charged Dorothy with first- degree murder. The defense responded with the same Jazzmania madness defense.

Interest in the case had subsided somewhat, and courtroom seats were "filled with a motley assortment of housewives, painted flappers, old men and young ones." During the trial, Dorothy was more subdued and seemed more a spectator than a participant. After ten days of dueling psychiatric testimony, the case went to the jury. The jury found Dorothy guilty of Manslaughter, and she was sentenced to 1 to 10 years in San Quentin. She seemed relieved with the verdict and was a cooperative and penitent convict.

In 1932, Dorothy was used as an example in "Science's Newest Evidence that Family Love May Cause Crime," an SF Chronicle article which claimed that Dorothy's parents' permissive attitude contributed to her crime.

She was released in 1932 after 7 years in San Quentin -- women, as well as men, were imprisoned there at the time -- and tried to slip into obscurity. But this was not to be. She was arrested in 1933, under the name of Dorothy Jentoff, for stealing $600 worth of cash, clothes, and jewelry from her roommate in order to go to a fancy party. The case made headlines again, and a distraught Dorothy tried to commit suicide. The roommate dropped the charges. Dorothy disappeared again from the public eye.

In 1936, she married and had two children with Robert Stafford, who she later divorced. In 1955, thirty years after the murder, her criminal habits caught up with her again.

As Diane Stafford, she was arrested for stealing $2,000 worth of cash, clothes, and jewelry from a former employer. Her 17-year-old son, Robert Stafford Jr., learned his family history for the first time. It was a history that he was repeating; he had been arrested for burglary and was in the same jail as his mother. She died on September 16, 1968, at the age of 59.

Paul Drexler

Forty-three years earlier, on the floor next to her mother's body was this verse:

> *Let the old life be covered by the new*
> *The old past so full of bad mistakes*
> *Let it be wholly hidden by the new*
> *By deeds as white as silent flakes*

The Duchess

March's Women's History Month honored pioneers like architect Julia Morgan and labor organizer Dolores Huerta, who blazed a path into male-dominated professions. But another female pioneer is rarely mentioned: Juanita "Duchess" Spinelli, the first woman to be executed in California.

Born in Kentucky in 1889, Juanita said that she was the daughter of a 14-year-old Indian princess who died in childbirth. She also claimed a background as a professional wrestler, a madam, and as an associate of Detroit's Purple Gang. It is difficult to separate fact from fiction in her biography since Juanita's relationship to the truth was as a distant cousin twice removed.

Juanita and her children, Lorraine and Joseph, led a nomadic life as they hitchhiked from place to place. She worked as a waitress in Texas, operated a gambling booth in a Salt Lake City carnival, and raised sheep during a short-lived marriage in Idaho. Juanita returned to Texas, deposited her children in an orphanage, and traveled to Mexico with Anthony Spinelli, a Detroit bank robber who was killed during a smuggling operation. Juanita then returned to Texas with a new child and moved the family to Detroit. Lorraine ran away to San Francisco to escape her domineering mother.

A disagreement with Motor City mobsters forced Juanita to leave town. Juanita took her sons and her new partner, 31-year-old Mike Simeone, and joined

Lorraine in San Francisco. Using Lorraine as a lure, Juanita attracted three dimwitted delinquents: Albert Ives, 23, Robert Sherrod, 18, and Gordon Hawkins, 21.

Juanita played the role of a modern-day Fagin as she conducted a crime school at her apartment at 1421 Golden Gate Avenue, about two blocks away from San Francisco's fabled Painted Ladies. Instead of teaching her charges how to pick pockets, she taught them how to roll drunks, steal cars and hold up gas stations.

A woman of many talents, Juanita could sew a blackjack together out of leather and lead and hit a poker chip with a knife at 15 feet. Her admiring acolytes called her "The Duchess."

Her child-rearing practices were unusual, to say the least. She used her daughter as bait to attract mugging victims and kept her young sons informed about the gang's shady activities. "I don't believe in keeping anything from children," she said. Of course, she did have her limits. "I don't believe in too many cocktails for little chaps. One or two mild whiskeys are enough."

Her crime strategy was to have her gang commit weekly, small-scale holdups and car thefts and to stay under the police radar. She would plan the crimes, then collect the money and weapons after each caper.

This strategy came apart on April 8, 1940, when Albert Ives shot barbeque stand owner Leland S. Cash on Ocean Beach during a robbery. The killing shattered accomplice Robert Sherrod's fragile psyche, and he began to talk about the murder with people outside the gang.

Some in the gang wanted to silence his loose tongue with a bullet, but the kind-hearted Duchess had a gentler idea. "I kind of liked that boy and wanted it to be a mercy killing," she later testified. She drugged him unconscious; Sherrod was then dressed in a bathing suit and thrown into the Sacramento River where he drowned. Fearing he would be the next victim; Ives fled and revealed the gang's activities to police.

Police caught the gang quickly. All of them, except Juanita, confessed. The Duchess, with maternal instincts worthy of Livia Soprano, blamed Sherrod's murder on her daughter Lorraine.

Juanita's fate was sealed when the gun that killed Cash was found in her purse. Her partners, Simeone and Hawkins, were also sentenced to death. Ives was sent to a hospital for the criminally insane, and Lorraine was released. After several stays of execution, Spinelli went to San Quentin's gas chamber on November 21, 1941.

Women's history teaches us that pioneering women have to be better than their male competitors in order to succeed. The Duchess was a case in point. Clinton Duffy, the noted San Quentin Warden, described Juanita as "the coldest, hardest character, male or female, I have ever known."

Paul Drexler

The Grandma from Hell

Iva was not a person who immediately stood out. She was middle-aged, short, with dull brown hair, dowdy clothes, and a kind of squint in one eye. But when she started talking, it was hard to take your ears off her. Iva produced a cascading stream of words and sentences, mostly about herself, about her psychic ability, her business savvy, and her health -- or lack of it. "I was in the jitney bus accident in San Francisco and I'm crippled. My bones are bad and my body is full of poison."

If you believed her, which was often difficult, you might think she'd be lucky to last out the year. She could say the most outrageous things with total belief. She was an oddball, you might think, but a harmless one -- until you saw her eyes behind the barrel of a gun and you realized how evil and crazy, she really was. Iva was a psychopath's psychopath.

She first came to Santa Rosa detective John Coffman's attention in December 1961 when he was asked to investigate the disappearance of a Santa Rosa motel owner named Mildred Arneson. Mildred was a nurse who had become a successful real estate investor. She lived at the Rose City Motor Hotel with her ex-husband, Jay, a retired Army Major, disabled with Parkinson's disease. Mildred, a Rosicrucian, had told her family that she was going to South America with a fellow spiritualist named Iva Long.

When Coffman went to the motel, he found that Iva Long was running it and that she had changed its name to the El Sombrero Motel. Iva confirmed that Mildred was somewhere in South America, but she denied that she had ever planned to accompany Mildred on her trip. She said she was taking care of Mildred's husband, Jay, until Mildred returned. Iva claimed to be a psychic and astrologer and offered to foretell Coffman's future if he gave her a lock of his hair. Although Iva's wild stories made Coffman suspicious, the deed transferring the motel to Ida Long appeared to be genuine, and the investigation stalled.

Mildred's Arneson's sister called Iva in January and she asked to speak to Jay Arneson, who was confined to a wheelchair. In a trembling voice, Jay said: "I don't think I'll ever see Mildred again." There was a moment of silence, then Iva spoke and said, "Don't pay any attention to him. Jay has been horribly upset ever since Mildred left here in such a hurry." Then she hung up. Jay Arneson disappeared in February. Iva said he had been picked up by two Mexicans in a Cadillac and taken to a nursing home somewhere in Southern California.

Coffman continued his investigation, calling Iva every day. Jay's sons hired a lawyer to look into their father's disappearance, and Mildred's sister made numerous trips to Santa Rosa to investigate.

In March, Mildred's mother received a letter from Mildred, sent from Tijuana, Mexico. The letter asked her to "stop meddling in our affairs" and said that Mildred wanted nothing more to do with her family. The FBI investigated and declared the letter a fake.

The investigation picked up steam in May when Iva had a dispute with a businessman trying to collect an overdue bill. The man, Herb Willsmore, told a story that revealed a different side of Iva. While Willsmore was installing a $2,400 water softening system for the motel, he became impressed by Iva's stories of her business acumen. She convinced him to loan her an additional $2,500 as part of a complex transaction in which he would receive a larger amount of blue-chip stocks which he could use as collateral to expand his business. Herb soon discovered that the stock purchase order she gave him was a forgery. When he demanded his money back, she led him on a circuitous and fruitless hunt for the money in bank vaults from San Francisco to Sacramento, and finally to Pine Bluffs, Wyoming.

Iva slipped away in Cheyenne. Willsmore returned alone, angry, and determined to collect his money. He drove to the motel with his wife and asked her to wait. Willsmore was ushered into a back room by two of Iva's employees. Iva was seated behind the desk. When he sat down, she raised a gun from under the desk and pointed it at his heart.

"Sign these forms," Iva demanded. On the desk was a receipt marked "Paid in Full." "What if I don't?" he replied. "We'll carry you out of here feet first and no one will ever know what happened to you," said Iva. Willsmore was saved when his wife knocked at the door. Thinking fast, Willsmore said it was the police. Iva quickly left the room. Willsmore called the police, but when they arrived, Iva denied having a gun, and her employees backed her up. As police began to take everyone to the station, Iva slipped out the back door, took a cab and disappeared. Police then searched the motel and found the gun.

Officers soon learned that Iva Long was an alias. Her real name was Iva Kroeger, born in Kentucky in 1919. She had been married at least three times. Iva also had a police record as a small- time grifter going back almost 20 years. As Paula Marie Pearson, she had been arrested in 1945 for impersonating a lieutenant in the Navy Nurse Corps. In 1947, as Lucille Byrd, Iva had stolen $1,400 from a nursing home in San Jose and had used aliases in various scams over the years. Iva had been married to Ralph Kroeger, a tight-lipped, dour man seventeen years her senior, since 1954. They owned a house at 490 Ellington Avenue in San Francisco.

Iva was the master of the sob story. She often wore a fake cast on her leg, told people that she had leukemia, and that she was going blind. Iva talked the owner of a purebred puppy into giving it to her after claiming that it was for a crippled, 7-year-old orphan. She then sold the dog for $50. But it was the streetcar accident, for which Iva was suing the bus company for $100,000, that was the central feature of her life. She and Ralph had moved to Santa Rosa to avoid insurance investigators and their creditors. But Iva had disappeared, and police were searching for her. They staked out race tracks and astrologers because of Iva's fondness for gambling and spiritualism.

Police tracked down her son in Fort Myers, Florida, and he told them an alarming story: Posing as Paula Shoemaker, a wealthy widow and motel owner from San Diego, Iva offered him a job in her motel and volunteered to take his small boys, age 3 and 4, for an overnight. Then she and the boys disappeared. A nationwide search for the trio began.

Iva's husband, Ralph, who was living in their house on Ellington Avenue, seemed unaware of Iva's whereabouts. He was surprised to learn that Iva had stolen $8,000 from their joint account. Police learned in August that Iva had hired a handyman to dig a hole in the basement of her home. Suspicious, police got a search warrant and began excavating the basement. After hours of digging, police uncovered a foot, then the body of Major Jay Arneson. Near him, in a trunk, was the body of Mildred Arneson. "I didn't know there was anybody down here," Ralph protested. Police arrested Ralph on suspicion of murder.

The case became even stranger when Iva's grandchildren were found wandering the streets in Oakland where she had abandoned them. The boys looked at photos of Ralph and Iva and identified them as "Grandma and Grandpa." They said that Iva had told them their parents had been killed in a car accident, and she was taking care of them. After this, Iva had a new nickname: "The Grandma from Hell."

Iva next surfaced in San Diego, where she told a couple handing out Jehovah's Witness booklets that she was a poor widow and was taking care of her 12-year-old daughter. The couple was taken in at first, but when they noticed her resemblance to the photos of Iva in the newspapers, they contacted the FBI. The feds arrested Iva as she was slipping out of her apartment.

When Iva was questioned about the bodies in the Ellington Avenue house, she claimed that a blackmailer was responsible. She claimed, "I've paid him $40,000 over the years so he wouldn't tell my husband about my police record." Iva and Ralph were charged with murder.

The Kroegers' defense team had an almost impossible task. When two bodies are found buried in cement in the basement of your house, it is hard to blame the murders on an intruder. The defense argued that Ralph Kroeger was innocent because he didn't know anything about the killings. And that although Iva was responsible for the deaths, she was not legally guilty by reason of insanity. Iva once told someone, "If you act crazy, you can get away with anything because people will think you are eccentric." This became her courtroom strategy.

The presiding judge was Harry Neubarth. He must have wondered what legal god he had offended to be given such an accursed trial.

A courtroom normally has strict rules of behavior. You speak when you're spoken to. No one talks except the attorneys, the witnesses, and the judge, and the judge is the final authority, like the captain of a ship. Iva broke every rule. She did whatever she wanted, whenever she wanted. She interrupted and argued with the witnesses, attorneys, and the judge. She threw things, sang, and fell asleep in the middle of the trial.

Excerpts from the trial transcript present some vivid examples.

DEFENDANT IVA KROEGER: Quiet. The master's got a headache.

THE COURT (Judge Neubarth): You know, Mrs. Kroeger, if you would stop talking over there, my headache would go away.

DEFENDANT IVA KROEGER: Have you really got a headache, your honor?

THE COURT (Judge Neubarth): I do because you're talking so much. Just be quiet for a second.

DEFENDANT IVA KROEGER: Put a cold rag on it. I'll put a cool rag on your head (turning to the audience), he's got a headache, an awful headache.

PROSECUTOR: This is part of the pattern, the bizarre conduct of the defendant. This is part of the defense.

THE COURT: That might come out when the doctors [psychiatrists] testify.

DEFENDANT IVA KROEGER: What doctors are you talking about?

PROSECUTOR: It is hearsay and self-serving to this individual.

DEFENDANT IVA KROEGER: Everything to you is hearsay.

Later in the trial, Iva interrupts her cross-examination by the prosecutor:

DEFENDANT IVA KROEGER: Oh, shut up. You shut up until I'm finished talking. And you respect the Mother of God.

THE COURT (Judge Neubarth): Now Mrs. Kroeger, listen. I told you yesterday that you were not doing your case any good.

DEFENDANT IVA KROEGER: I'm telling the truth. I can't remember names. I even went upstairs with such a severe headache, and if it wasn't for the girls putting hot packs and giving me aspirins, and I was laying still, I couldn't even think straight. Because I don't remember a lot of things. I went once one time and got lost and was in Hawaii. It's not a funny situation. You needn't laugh.

THE PROSECUTOR: I think under the circumstances, I will conclude the cross-examination.

DEFENDANT IVA KROEGER: You ought to be ashamed of yourself. You are not a man. You're a gangster.

THE COURT (Judge Neubarth): I think we'll adjourn until tomorrow morning at 10:00 o'clock.

DEFENDANT IVA KROEGER (singing): "When Irish eyes are smiling, it's like the morning spring. When Irish eyes are smiling, they'll surely steal your heart away."

The doctor, a psychiatrist, gave Iva's act a poor review. He testified that she was deceitful and manipulative but legally sane. "I found her to be what I would call a diabolical liar on the grounds that she shows cunning, ingenuity, cruelty, wickedness, cold calculations, evil conduct and intent."

Defense attorneys in hopeless cases often concoct new theories, even if these theories conflict with their previous ones. Like saying, "My client absolutely did not commit the murders. And if she did, she was legally insane at the time." The final defense witness was an 80-pound bag of cement. In an attempt to show that Iva lacked the strength to commit the murders, her lawyers had her try to lift the bag. In a Herculean effort that puts to shame O.J. Simpson attempts to fit the glove on his hand, Iva struggled mightily. She grimaced and the strain on her face was evident, but alas, she could not move the bag.

The jury was unimpressed. Iva was convicted and sentenced to death. She won a new trial on the grounds that Judge Neubarth erred in telling the jurors that a life sentence can be as little as seven years. Iva was convicted again in 1964, and this time Judge Neubarth sentenced her to life imprisonment. "When I say life, I mean it. Psychiatrists say she should never be returned to society. I shall file a separate report saying that in no circumstances should she ever be released from prison," the judge added, calling the case "the most gruesome crime I have ever tried."

Iva was sent to Corona Women's Prison, but the indefatigable grandma wasn't finished hustling. In 1966, the Santa Rosa Press Democrat published an article entitled "Iva Kroeger Going Blind in Prison," reporting that "she continues to shuffle through her days using crutches, using the vision of but one eye, aided by a heavy lens."

In 1971, the San Francisco Chronicle published an article entitled "Prison Poetess Iva Kroeger," which reported that Iva was writing poetry for a prison newsletter. Quoting the newsletter, the Chronicle reporter wrote: "The thing we like most about Iva is that not only has she overcome her physical handicaps, but she's not allowed herself to become bitter or spiritually defeated by the time she's done. She can still find a moment of beauty to share, a helping hand to offer."

Iva was the picture of cooperation and rehabilitation in prison. Her good behavior and California's determinate sentencing law won her parole to Riverside, California, in 1975. She was declared legally blind, became a Scientologist, and took courses in sociology at UC Riverside. She continued to claim her innocence.

Her parole ended in 1980, and she told people she planned to go to nursing school. In the mid-1980s, Iva periodically visited her brothers in Florida. In 1986, Eda Weitzel, a registered nurse from San Diego, met Iva on a bus going from Missouri to California. Calling herself Paula Schoonmaker, Iva claimed to be a wealthy nurse who owned real estate in California. She hired Eda as a personal assistant, and they both stopped in Las Vegas to gamble. Iva disappeared after stealing Weitzel's identification; and, posing as Weitzel, she landed a series of jobs in Florida nursing facilities.

Iva then learned that her nephew's 18-month-old son had drowned in a swimming pool. Iva became inconsolable and blamed Andy Pitcher, her nephew's business partner, for the child's death. She said that

Pitcher was forcing her nephew to spend long hours at work and reasoned that if her nephew had been at home, he would have prevented his baby's death. She called Pitcher and threatened to kill him and his family, adding, "If you don't believe, me check the records. I've killed before." A policeman questioned her, but she conned him and even got him to give her a ride to her place. She called Pitcher again telling him," I'm an old woman and I've already served 16 years in prison, and the only thing I haven't decided is how I'm going to kill you." When police realized who she was, they came looking for her, but she had already left the area.

Iva was last sighted in 1989 while shopping in a Santa Rosa department store. She died in Massachusetts in 2000.

Isabella J. Martin, The Queen of Grudges

If "holding grudges" was an Olympic event, Isabella Martin would have won the gold medal. For 15 years, she was the bane of the Northern California legal fraternity. Just the sight of her in a courtroom was enough to send seasoned attorneys screaming into the night. But her extralegal activities were even more frightening.

Born Isabella Bidwell in New York State in 1861, she moved to Weaverville, California, a gold mining town, in 1890 to go husband prospecting after divorcing her first spouse. She struck gold when she married 58-year-old John Martin, a wealthy mine owner. Isabella went to New York in 1891 and returned with a baby she named "Baby John Martin" after his father. But Isabella's irascible disposition soon alienated the townspeople.

When John Martin died in 1892, Isabella reached out to John's wealthier brother, Henry, claiming that the people of Weaverville were conspiring against her and her two-year-old son. Henry Martin, however, wanted nothing to do with her. He suspected Isabella of killing his brother and didn't believe that John was the father of Isabella's son.

When Henry died in 1893, Isabella sued his estate on behalf of her son. According to Isabella, she and Henry had a very close secret relationship, implying that Henry was the father of "Baby John." She produced letters he had written to her along with a second will which she claimed that Henry had written just before he died. In ~~it,~~ the will, Henry gave his beloved nephew, "Baby John" Martin, one-third of his estate. The sensational three-month battle over Henry's estate became the Bay Area's hottest ticket. "Baby John" was a constant presence in the courtroom, and he was doted over by both sides. Isabella added a note of glamour by wearing a fashionable new dress each day of the trial.

Isabella loved the spotlight and would make outlandish comments to the press; She told a reporter that she had fired Crittenden Thornton, one of her attorneys, for "writing her letters of too friendly a nature." This was news to attorney Thornton, who emphatically denied the allegations and resigned from the case. During another tantrum, Isabella threw a civil code law book at a lawyer's head. As a result of Isabella's behavior, a policeman was stationed in front of Judge Coffey's desk "to prevent Mrs. John from biting Attorney Delmas or otherwise inflicting great bodily injury upon the person of that gentleman."

Arthur Rodgers, the opposing attorney, shredded Isabella's reputation. He introduced extortion letters that Isabella had written to wealthy Andrew Crawford claiming that Crawford was the father of her child. Witnesses testified that Henry Martin was too sick to have written the will, and handwriting experts testified that her letters and Henry's second will were forgeries. Rodgers even cast doubt on Isabella's maternal claim by showing that she was betting at the racetrack just the day before she allegedly gave birth.

With virtually no evidence on Isabella's side, her attorney, Grove L. Johnson, fell back on his oratorical skills. He told the jury that it didn't really matter if Henry was the child's father, and praised his client's lack of greed, saying she was only asking for about a third of the contested fortune.

Referring to the biblical story of Saul and the witch of Endor, he said: "Had I had the power of the witch of Endor, I would summon him here. I can almost hear the air rustle with her presence. Give Baby John his fortune. Give him the fortune I would have given him and right the wrong I have given him."

Unsurprisingly, the jury ruled against Isabella. The vengeful woman lost her case and immediately set out to make the life of attorney Rodgers as miserable as possible. She wrote Roger's fiancée, saying: "I shall watch the career of yourself and husband with great interest and fervor, for Arthur Rodgers can never, while life lasts, undertake or attempt anything that will not be closely followed by myself." She filed two $500,000 lawsuits in 1898 against Rodgers for defamation of character on behalf of herself and "Baby John".

Isabella was in court almost continually over the next twelve years. She was arrested for threatening an actor's life and for trying to evict her tenants with an ax. She was sued for non-payment by numerous hotels, grocers, lumber dealers, and the Bay District Race Track. She also initiated many lawsuits, often acting as her own attorney.

Two of Isabella's Oakland cottages burned down in 1901, followed by a number of suspicious fires in the area. The Westchester Fire Insurance Company refused her claim on the grounds that the fire was arson. Isabella sued and the case was assigned to Judge Frank Ogden. The case went on for years and was dismissed in 1905. Dissatisfied, Isabella went east and threatened the life of the president of the insurance company. In 1907, Judge Ogden's home was partially destroyed by a mysterious dynamite blast.

The next year the mystery was solved. Sixteen-year-old "Baby John" was arrested in Weaverville for setting fire to a barn. While in jail, John made a horrifying confession to his jailor. Under his mother's orders, he had burned her cottages for the insurance and bombed Judge Ogden's house. In addition, he and his mother had constructed bombs to blow up the houses of the head of the Contra Water Company and a police judge. They had dynamited an irrigation ditch, burned a barn, poisoned a sugar barrel in a grocery store, and attempted to kill the inhabitants of Weaverville by poisoning their water supply. Fortunately, the current flowed the other way and only some animals were poisoned.

For six years, "Baby John," under constant beatings and death threats from his mother, had become the instrument for settling her many grudges. He showed authorities numerous caches of explosives that he and his mother had hidden.

Isabella was arrested and put on trial for the bombing of Judge Ogden's house. She admitted that her son was adopted. Isabella then showed her true maternal feelings by blaming everything on her son and called him a "degenerate. John has never had anything but good advice from me," she claimed. "He has been insane from his early youth," she added. Isabella blamed all the crimes on her son's heredity.

Isabella conducted her defense with her usual fury while her court-appointed lawyers competed to see who could sit farthest away from their client. Almost all the witnesses she called for her defense ended up testifying against her. Despite days of fierce cross-examination, John's story remained intact. Other witnesses testified to Isabella's mistreatment of John. She even broke his nose, they said. It took the jury only six minutes to declare her guilty and she was sentenced to life imprisonment.

Although she was in prison, Isabella maintained her reputation as a fashionista. "Mrs. Isabella J. Martin is very anxious to have a good picture of herself put in the rogues' gallery. She made the photographer pose her three times after she had made a very careful toilet. When he showed her a proof of the picture, she was very well satisfied," reported the San Francisco Call.

During her appeal in 1910, she explained to the judge that she wore men's trousers while at home in Weaverville because it was in keeping with the prevailing fashion. "I am surprised at your ignorance. Don't you know that in Europe and in other centers of fashion women wear what is known as touring trousers? I was not wearing men's clothing or attempting to disguise myself. I was only wearing the latest fashion. Why John Pierpont Morgan's daughter wears them."

Isabella managed to get a new trial, but the verdict was the same. She added more histrionics by attempting suicide in court. After saying, "I will not go back to jail. I will die right here," she slit her wrists with broken glass.

Freed of his mother's domination, John returned to Weaverville and emerged as a popular honor student. The nickname "Baby" John followed him into adulthood. He became a miner upon graduation and managed what was left of his mother's properties.

Isabella's time in prison did nothing to soften her temper. She threw hot soup on one matron and kicked another into unconsciousness. She filed constant appeals to the courts. In 1914, she was committed to Napa State Mental Hospital where she died in 1929.

SERIAL KILLERS

Why are we so fascinated by serial killers? Why do they do it? Is there a part of us that is both thrilled and horrified by people who violate our deepest taboos? Is there a logical explanation for their actions or is there just evil in the world?

The FBI defines a serial killer as a person who commits at least two separate murders, with a cooling off period. Many serial killers suffer from psychopathy, which is defined as a personality disorder marked by extreme egocentricity and antisocial behavior. These monsters are psychopaths, a word that seems to vibrate with excitement and danger. Psychopaths can be charming, cold-hearted, ruthless, fearless, irresponsible, impulsive, and deadly.

Even the brains of psychopaths are different. Neuroscientists have identified three parts of the brain -- the amygdala, the frontal lobe, and the cerebral cortex -- that differ between the normal and the psychopathic brain. Psychopaths are desensitized to violence and cruelty. Brain scans of the cerebral cortex, which regulates memory and self-awareness, and the frontal lobe, which is responsible for self-control and judgment, show much less activity in psychopaths. So, they are less likely to remember their mistakes, control their behavior, or consider the risks before they act.

Though most serial killers are psychopaths, by no means are most psychopath serial killers, or even criminals. Being egotistical, bold, selfish, superficially charming, and cunning can be extremely valuable in getting ahead, and a surprisingly large percentage of business leaders, attorneys and politicians score high in tests for psychopathy. In one famous case, James Fallon, a prominent Neuroscientist who was studying the brain scans of psychopathic murderers, discovered that his own brain shared the same characteristics.

In TV, books, and movies, serial killers are often inaccurately portrayed as physically grotesque or as criminal geniuses. Only two of our serial killers, Earle Nelson, who was known as the Gorilla Killer, and Alfred Cline, who killed so cleverly that he was never tried for murder, come close to fitting these descriptions. Our San Francisco serial killers come from a wide range of backgrounds; from dirt poor and oppressed to filthy rich and privileged. Welcome to San Francisco's serial killers, the best of our worst.

The Terror Bandits

The Crimes

The reign of the Terror Bandits began with a gun and ended with a scalpel. "1 Dead, 3 Hurt as Robbers Spread Terror," screamed the headlines in the San Francisco Chronicle.

On October 9, 1926, two men began a crime spree men by stealing a car at 1350 Vallejo Street on San Francisco's Russian Hill. They invaded a pool hall on Lombard Street and robbing eight men, shooting two of them in the process. They next drove across town to 17th and Missouri where they accosted two men. The bandits recognized the men as fellow criminals, and, citing professional courtesy, left them alone.

During the next forty minutes, they robbed two cabbies and two pedestrians at gunpoint. As police responded to the crimes, the bandits moved into the South of Market district. At 8th and Bryant streets, the robbers accosted a group including Mrs. Emma Bird and her 13-year-old daughter. They dragged Mrs. Bird into the car and drove off. She told them she was the mother of ten children and pleaded with them to let her go. Two blocks farther after flashing a light in her face and deciding, "She ain't young enough," they threw her from the automobile.

The auto bandits then doubled back down to Fifth Street and Harrison, where they pistol- whipped and robbed two more victims, then stole the evening's receipts from a Lombard Street poolroom, shooting two patrons in the process. But they were just getting started.

Crossing back over Market Street, they drove to Powell and Washington streets where they accosted Mario Pagano. When Pagano resisted and started running, they shot him down. The shots drew the attention of San Francisco Police Chief Dan O'Brien, who was leaving a dinner party down the street. O'Brien and his chauffeur Sergeant Neely found Pagano dying in the street and exchanged shots with the bandits. The killers robbed three more people before ending their six- hour crime spree at 2:30 a.m. In all, the pair held up 23 people in fourteen different robberies. Their total take was about $400 and assorted pieces of jewelry. Ten hours later, police recovered the stolen car but had little to go on other than a description of two young white males.

Two days later, on a Monday, the terror began again. Two men flagged down Walter Swanson, a Yellow Cab driver, murdered him at 16th and Third streets and tossed his body under a viaduct. One of the bandits put on the driver's cap and jacket, and using Swanson's cab, they drove to Mariposa Street in the Potrero District where they stopped and asked a man for the time. When the man took out his watch, they shot him to death. The killers continued their spree on nearby Mississippi Street, robbing two men, and then held up a restaurant on Brannon Street, shooting one of the diners. The holdup men crossed the street to a gas station where they murdered the night watchman and wounded two of his friends. The killers continued their spree on Potrero Hill where they robbed nine more people, killing one of them. They plundered the pockets of a sailor at Pier 37.

They were holding up a man at a gas station when Officer Dorsey Henderson drove up. A running gun battle ensued which ended at 16th and Mississippi, where the killers smashed the cab into the curb. They fled through a lumberyard, stole another car, and disappeared down the Bayshore highway. The entire rampage was over in less than an hour. Chief O'Brien ordered the mobilization of the entire police department. Supplemented by volunteers, the force of 2,000 men was soon patrolling the streets with orders to "shoot to kill."

Teams of detectives worked tirelessly over the next week as police blanketed the city. Detectives Waffer and De Matei got a tip from an underworld source: "We can't say who gave it to us because the gang might try to hide a little hot lead under his skin" said Waffer. "All we had to go on was a description of one of the killers." His name was Lawrence Weeks. When the detectives confronted him, Weeks confessed and said his partner on the Saturday night crime spree was 22-year-old Clarence "Buck" Kelly. But he denied being with Kelly during the Monday night holdups.

"Buck" Kelly, a sometimes cabdriver and club boxer, was a well-known South of Market thug with a criminal record dating back to age 16. In April 1926, he was arrested for rape; his case was pending at the time of the murders.

*Buck Kelly's crime spree panicked
San Francisco in 1926.
(San Francisco Examiner)*

Police surrounded the apartment at 47 South Park where Kelly lived with his family. As Kelly tried to escape down the back stairs, he was shot twice by detectives and taken to San Francisco General Hospital in critical condition. He refused an operation, stating, "I want to die right now. I don't want to live and have the cops hang me."

Kelly admitted nothing, and angrily referred to Weeks as a "squealer." Hundreds of angry cab drivers, many of them World War I veterans, plotted to lynch Kelly, but a squad of heavily armed police foiled the mob.

Police soon arrested a third man, 17-year- old Michael Papadaches, after tracking him down at a Waller Street speakeasy. According to Papadaches, the Monday murder spree started out as a quest for revenge. On the Saturday evening after the first murders, Kelly went out drinking and got into a fight with a longshoreman over a woman. The longshoreman KOed Kelly with one punch. Furious, Kelly got his gun and went looking for revenge. He met Papadaches at the speakeasy on Monday, and after drinking heavily for an hour, the pair began their murderous spree.

The Punishment

After indicting the three men, the grand jury urged the passing of a national bill to restrict the sale and use of firearms, citing the ease in which the bandits procured their weapons.

Kelly testified at his trial that he had suffered cranial injuries during his childhood, including being kicked in the mouth by a horse. He also said he had been a heavy drinker since the age of 16, and that when drinking he often suffered from blackouts. Kelly claimed that he could remember nothing about the crimes and denied ever owning or firing a gun. His defense lawyer argued that the combination of brain injuries and drinking rendered Kelly insane at the time of the crimes.

The defense argument crumbled in the face of Dr. Joseph Catton's expert psychiatric testimony. Catton said that Kelly's skull was intact; he had suffered no permanent brain injuries and did not have amnesia. "It is my belief that he knew at all times what he was doing and knows now everything that he did."

The evidence against Kelly was overwhelming. His gun was matched to the killings; numerous eyewitnesses identified him, and his co-defendant, Michael Papadaches, testified against him. After only 30 minutes of deliberation, the jury found Kelly guilty on three counts of first-degree murder. He was sentenced to death and sent to San Quentin.

In May of 1927, his father, John Kelly, was arrested for robbing and beating the owner of a Chinese lottery. John Kelly attempted suicide in jail and had to be restrained by five guards. He was convicted and sent to San Quentin. Neither the father nor the son ever requested to see the other while housed in the same prison.

Kelly's lawyers initiated another appeal, and Buck Kelly was moved back to San Francisco county jail. On September 11, 1927, Kelly and four other prisoners attempted a jailbreak. Two of the prisoners, "Creepy" Wilson and William De Bardeleben, were associates of Joe Tanko, the infamous escape artist and murderer who had been killed in a shootout with San Francisco police in November 1926. The men staged a fight with another prisoner. When guards came to break up the fight, the prisoners turned on them and tried to escape. Additional guards foiled the escape, and the men were put in solitary confinement. Kelly's appeal was denied.

Exactly eight months later, on May 11, 1928, Buck Kelly was hanged in San Quentin.

But the unkindest cut of all was to come at the hands of Dr. Leo Stanley. Stanley, San Quentin's Chief Surgeon for 40 years, was a man of contradictions. Unlike most prison "sawbones," Stanley was a first-rate surgeon who helped to modernize prison medicine. He was also a eugenicist who performed thousands of operations on prisoners that would be considered unethical or illegal today.

Dr. Stanley removed Kelly's testicles, which were later implanted into an older man.

This cutting-edge procedure known as "gland therapy" was first discovered by Serge Voronoff, who while he had been a physician in the court of the king of Egypt, treated the court eunuchs. Voronoff hypothesized that maintaining active genital glands was the secret to health and conducted animal experiments. He went on to transplant bits of monkey testes into aging men. He claimed success, although he could offer no scientific validation of his claim.

But the Goat Gland King was "Doctor" J.R. Brinkley. Brinkley, a former snake-oil salesman who purchased his medical degree from a diploma mill, established a phenomenally successful gland transplant business. Brinkley bought a 50,000-watt radio station in 1924 and became a pioneer in radio advertising, pitching his goat gland business to a national audience. Charging $750 a transplant -- $10,000 in today's money -- Brinkley became fabulously wealthy. His claim that his procedure could cure diseases such as insanity, influenza, and acne brought him into conflict with the American Medical Association, which stripped him of his medical license.

In order to get his license back, Brinkley ran as a write-in candidate to be governor of Kansas in 1930 and came close to winning. Brinkley eventually lost his fortune to government actions and lawsuits by former patients who died or became ill from his treatments. He died penniless in 1942.

Dr. Stanley's fate was much different. Though Dr. Stanley sterilized thousands of inmates and implanted goat glands into many of them, the media routinely praised him. It was a time when eugenics, or selective breeding, was seen as a way to improve society and reduce crime. There was a scandal when the removal of Buck Kelly's organs became public knowledge, though many came to Dr. Stanley's defense. The San Francisco Examiner supported Dr. Stanley in an editorial entitled "San Quentin's Valuable Work for Science Should Continue," and the furor died down.

Earle Nelson: The Dark Strangler

Earle Nelson admiring his strangling hands.
(San Francisco Examiner 1927)

The first landlady died on February 20, 1926. Sixty-year-old Clara Newman was last seen showing a man an attic apartment in her home on Pierce Street in San Francisco. Mertin Newman, her nephew, found her strangled and violated body in the attic two hours later. Mertin described the man as around 30 years old, with a dark complexion, average height, and a stocky build.

A similar murder occurred just two weeks later. Laura Beal, a 65-year-old landlady, was strangled in San Jose. The two killings were eerily similar: Both women were aging landladies showing a room, and both were strangled and killed in the afternoon. Witnesses said the killer, soon to be labeled the

Strangler, had a dark complexion, was of medium height, and had a stocky build. But there was another, more horrifying, connection between the killings that was only hinted at to the public. The attacker was a necrophiliac. Both women had been sexually assaulted after death.

Though no one could have imagined it at the time, the two killings were the first courses in a movable feast of murder that would extend through two countries, 13 cities and the murders of 22 women.

On June 10, the Strangler struck again in San Francisco, killing Lillian St. Mary, age 63, who was showing an apartment on Delores Street. "The San Francisco police have had no one like him to contend with in the whole history of the city," said the newspapers.

Just two weeks later, Mrs. Ollie Russell was strangled in Santa Barbara and her jewelry was taken. Her body showed the same abuse as the other victims. Fear gripped the region. This was something new. Never had there been a murderer who killed in this way; who moved from place to place.

More descriptions of the killer surfaced. The man had watery blue eyes, a piercing stare, large hands, and a "ghastly smile" on his face. The newspapers called him "The Dark Strangler" or the "Dark Fiend." "No woman in San Francisco is safe with this man at large," declared Police Chief Donald J. O'Brien. The descriptions made the Strangler seem almost like a monster. But he wasn't. People who met him described his "ingratiating manner." Others said he carried a Bible and seemed very religious.

Additional reports of attacks came from all over the West. Police searched mental hospital records, looking for a recent release or escape.

Then, in August, there was a break in the case. Philip Brown, who was picked up as a vagrant in Needles, California, confessed to killing the four women. Brown was brought to San Bernardino where police had a witness. William Franey, a Los Angeles fireman, identified Brown as the killer of Ollie Russell -- but it was a very unusual identification. Franey claimed to have seen the attack on Mrs. Russell as he peeked through a keyhole in the door. Police put Brown in a room and had Franey peer through the keyhole. He then identified Brown as Mrs. Russell's attacker.

Brown had a history of epilepsy and violent attacks and had spent time at the state mental hospital in San Bernardino. The police chief and district attorney of that Southern California city were convinced they had the right man. Still, there were some doubts. The suspect was described as stocky, but Brown was thin. Police who questioned him wondered about his mental condition. As the days went on, Brown's story unraveled. He was declared incompetent and sent to a mental hospital.

The search continued. The Strangler moved north to Portland, murdering three landladies in five days. Hysteria increased. Santa Cruz police arrested a stocky foreigner after three women were assaulted. A lynch mob threatened him until Mertin Newman said that he was not the person who killed his aunt.

Any dark-skinned, stocky, Mediterranean type who fit the general description was a suspect. George

Wininski, Orin Decius, Steve Kelimas, and others were all arrested. Almost every day there were reports of attacks by the Strangler. It couldn't be just one person. Other criminals seemed to be jumping on the Strangler bandwagon.

On November 18, Nelson returned to San Francisco and strangled Mrs. William Edwards, who was showing a house for sale at 3524 Fulton Street. He took her jewelry and left her naked body under the bed. The next day in Burlingame, a suburb south of the city, Mrs. Murray, eight months pregnant, was approached by a prospective buyer for her house. He spent more than an hour looking over the house, asking questions about its construction. Her caution saved her life. " I took care to keep six to eight feet away from him during the whole interview."

Then, when Mrs. Murray turned to open the front door, he attacked her. She fought back and, with desperate strength, raked her nails against his face and managed to make it to the street. He fled, but she was able to give police their first detailed description. "Description of Strangler Now Complete; Arrest Certain," read the headline in the November 22 edition of the San Francisco Chronicle. The headline was overly optimistic.

The Strangler again moved north to Oregon and Washington, killing a woman in each city. In December, he headed east. He killed Mrs. John Beard in Council Bluffs, Iowa, on December 23. He took a short break for Christmas, then killed Bonnie Pace in Kansas City on December 27. The next day, he killed and ravaged

Germania Harpin and her eight-month-old son. Then he disappeared again.

By 1927, the press had come up with a new name for the Strangler, "The Gorilla Killer," because of his big hands and simian posture." On April 27, 1927, he struck again in Philadelphia. In the May 1 edition of the Philadelphia Inquirer was an article, with three large photo illustrations entitled, "How to Escape from the Strangler."

On May 30, he struck in Buffalo as his murderous pace quickened. On June 1, he throttled two women in Detroit. On June 3, his victim was Mary Sietsma in Chicago. Police throughout the Midwest were on high alert. It was time for the Strangler to look for victims in new places. On June 5, he hitchhiked to Winnipeg, Canada, the third largest city in the country.

He got a job as a construction laborer and checked into a rooming house under the name of Roger Wilson. "I want quiet surroundings where I can reflect," he said. "A man with Christ in his heart need worry about nothing else." His landlady, Mrs. August Hill, was impressed with his piety.

On June 9, Lola Cowan disappeared as she sold artificial flowers on the street. It was her 14th birthday. The next day, the Strangler entered the rooming house of Emily Patterson and asked for a room. He said he didn't have any money but would do odd jobs to pay for his room. When her husband came home that evening, Emily was missing. Hours later, he discovered her body underneath their bed.

Police mobilized and started checking every boarding house in the city. When they reached Mrs. Hill's house, she described her tenant, Roger Wilson, as a short, dark, religious man. Police searched his room and found the decaying body of Lola Cowan under his bed. The city exploded. Thousands of sightings were reported to authorities.

A second-hand clothing dealer told police that the Strangler had been in his store and described his clothing. This description was broadcast throughout Canada.

The Manitoba Provincial Police came to help. In addition, hundreds of US police officers, including San Francisco's chief of detectives, who were heading for a police convention in Windsor, Ontario, went instead to Winnipeg to help with the search.

An all-points bulletin for Roger Wilson was broadcast over the radio and sent to all post offices and police stations in Manitoba. The special bulletin said: "The Strangler is an affable man, say those who had dealings with him. He is able to assume any role. He is well read." Police issued a special warning for all women with houses for sale or rooms to let.

The Strangler headed west towards Regina, the capital of the neighboring province of Saskatchewan. He rented a room in Regina from Mrs. Rowe and told her he might be staying for a week. The next morning, he bought Mrs. Rowe's nine-year-old daughter an ice cream cone and tried to lure her into a side street. She refused to go with him, a decision that undoubtedly saved her life.

By this time, he had been tracked to Regina, and searchers were pouring into the city. He doubled back into Manitoba and headed south. His money was running out. Authorities believed that the Strangler would try to return by train to the United States, which was only 100 miles south. Police sent descriptions to all police stations and post offices. "We especially ask all railway men, both passenger and freight crews, to help us catch this fiend, who is a degenerate of the worst type, and protect other defenseless women," they implored.

He was next sighted near Boissevain, 40 miles north of the border.

The speed at which the Strangler had moved and his ability to fade into the background had long frustrated police. But there were nothing but small prairie towns between Boissevain and the border. A hitchhiking stranger would be noticed. The odds were finally in the pursuers' favor. On June 15, Constable Grey of Killarney, a border town of 1,000, was notified about a stranger in town. The man, who gave his name as Virgil Wilson, agreed to come to the police station. Wilson was so relaxed and friendly that Grey could hardly believe he was the wanted man. Even so, the cautious Grey took away his belt, shoes and socks, locked him in a cell, and handcuffed him to the bars. He walked into the next room and called Inspector Smith in Winnipeg. "That's him! " Smith shouted. He used the name Wilson in Winnipeg. Don't let him out of your sight! " Inspector Smith assembled fifty police officers to go with him on a special train to Killarney.

When Grey returned to the jail, he found the cell door open and handcuffs dangling from the bar. Wilson had picked the locks with a nail file he found on the floor of the cell. Panic gripped the town. Most of the women and children in town spent the night in a church, guarded by dozens of armed men. A 500-man posse, equipped with rifles, axes and pitchforks went from house to house. "Virgil Wilson" spent a peaceful night hidden in the loft of a farmer's barn, just one block from the police station.

The next morning, as crowds searched for him, "Wilson" made his way towards the train station and waited for the train from Winnipeg that was heading toward the border. As the train pulled into town, he jumped out of this hiding place and made a break for the last car. A mob of people saw him and chased him. A constable grabbed him as he reached the station. The train doors opened and fifty constables, led by Inspector Smith, poured out of the train and engulfed the suspect. They took him onto the train and headed back to Winnipeg, avoiding the angry crowd that was intent on conducting Canada's first lynching.

By the time the train returned, the suspect had admitted his real name. It was not Virgil Wilson, nor was it Adrian Harris, the name under which he had strangled three women in Portland, the previous year. It was Earle Nelson, and he was from San Francisco.

Who was Earle Nelson?

If you wanted to create a serial killer, it would be hard to improve on the Earle Nelson recipe:

Start with a large dose of Venereal Disease

Earle was born in 1897. His mother died of syphilis when he was ten months old. Seven months later, his father also died of the disease. Venereal disease can affect parts of the brain

Simmer slowly with fire and brimstone religion

He lived with his grandmother and then with his Aunt. Both were strict Pentecostal Christians who constantly railed against the evils of sex and sins. Earle was a psychotic prodigy. He was expelled from primary school at the age of seven.

His strange behavior included talking to invisible people, quoting Bible passages about the great beast, and peeking at his cousin Rachel while she undressed. Though short, Earle developed large hands and tremendous upper body strength. He could walk on his hands for blocks at a time. He would show off by lifting chairs with his teeth. He was shunned by other children.

He would often leave the house with a new set of clothes and return days later dressed in dirty ragged clothing. Exchanging his clothing for other used clothing would become a life-long practice

Shake briskly and serve

At the age of 10, Earle was hit and dragged by a streetcar which cracked his skull and put him into a coma. The doctors didn't think he would survive. He regained consciousness after five days. But he was changed. He was subject to losses of memory and blinding headaches. A surprisingly high percentage of psychopaths have experienced serious head injuries.

Earle left school at 14, worked in a series of manual jobs, never staying in a job for long. He followed the family tradition by acquiring a venereal disease in the brothels of the Barbary Coast. By age 19, Earle had been in San Quentin, the Navy, and Napa State Mental Hospital. Upon being discharged from Napa State, he signaled an obsession with older women by marrying a fifty- eight-year-old Pentecostal spinster. She rejected his strong sexual demands, and he soon abandoned her.

After attacking a 12-year-old girl, Nelson was arrested and spent three more years in Napa State Mental Hospital, escaping three times. The authorities tired of his constant escapes, but rather than send him to a more secure place or continue to treat him, they gave up. And in a spectacular example of medical malpractice, doctors discharged Nelson in 1925, saying he was "improved." Nelson spent the rest of his life proving his doctors wrong.

The search for the Strangler occupied more police in more cities than any other case in history. At one time or another, the police forces of San Francisco, San Jose, Portland, Kansas City, Philadelphia, Detroit, Chicago, and Winnipeg had all been mobilized.

Nelson was convicted of murder and executed in Winnipeg on January 13, 1928. "May the Lord have mercy on my soul" were his last words.

The next day, landladies all over North America breathed a sigh of relief.

The Buttermilk Bluebeard

Buttermilk is the new black. This ancient drink, originally a by-product of making butter, is now a favorite of the artisan-food crowd. It is high in protein, easy to digest, and a natural treatment against gastrointestinal ailments. All in all, buttermilk is quite a healthy drink -- unless prepared and served by Alfred Cline. Cline, called a "fiendish philanderer" by the Syracuse Post Standard, poisoned as many as 11 people with buttermilk, but he was so clever that police were never able to charge him with murder.

Alfred Cline, the "Buttermilk Bluebeard,"
serves his last stretch in San Quentin.
(California State archives, 1947)

Cline, who was born in the Bible belt of Kansas in 1889, married early, had two children and gained a reputation as an upstanding farmer, Sunday school teacher, and choir member. In 1915, Cline moved his family to Fort Collins, Colorado, where he became a salesman and real estate operator. In 1929, Cline attempted to steal a rich widow's estate by forging her name on some legal documents. He was convicted of grand theft and sent to the Colorado penitentiary.

When he emerged in 1930, he added a deadly twist to his forgery practice and began earning a lethal living.

If Cline had a to-do list, it would have looked like this:

1. Find a rich old widow and marry her.

2. Take her to a hotel in another state.

3. Give her poisoned buttermilk.

4. Get the death certificate from the doctor.

5. Ship the body to another state and have it cremated.

6. Forge documents, collect her assets, and begin again.

He met and charmed 75-year-old Laura Cummings in Los Angeles. They decided to take a trip up the Pacific Coast. Somewhere along the way, Mrs. Cummings changed her will, leaving her $60,000 estate to Cline. She suddenly became ill in British Columbia and entered a hospital, where the doctors found she had been poisoned. By the time she recovered, Cline had decamped to Los Angeles. Her attorneys convinced a reluctant Mrs. Cummings to destroy the new will. "I hate to do this," she said. "He's such a sweet man."

Cline's future traveling companions were not so fortunate. He married Mrs. Carey Porter, another wealthy widow, a few months later. He proposed an auto trip and they drove to Reno. She died three weeks later, leaving him the sole heir to her $20,000 estate. Cline had her body shipped to Oakland and cremated.

Men, as well as women, were on the receiving end of the Cline buttermilk treatment. In 1931, Rev. Ernest Jones, a retired minister, met Cline and they took a trip together. Jones died of heart failure and heat prostration, leaving Cline $11,000. Jones's body was shipped to Glendale where it was cremated.

In 1932, Cline married Bessie Van Sickle, who was living with her brother-in-law, Lucas McCreary. They both expired within a few months, leaving Cline $21,200 in insurance and inheritance.

Cline miscalculated a year later, and Martin Frame, his next victim, survived. Frame told police that Cline had given him a glass of buttermilk. He also remembered signing some forms before he passed out.

Police searched Cline's luxurious home in Glendale and found Martin Frame's wallet, vials of barbiturate and cyanide, and will forms with Frame's signature on them. When the police found out about Cline's background, they investigated him for murder. But they couldn't find enough physical evidence to bring charges.

Instead, Alfred Cline was convicted of drugging and robbing Martin Frame and sentenced to 15 years in Folsom Prison. While there, Cline explained to his cellmate his preference for buttermilk. "If you want to poison someone, put it in buttermilk. The taste of buttermilk masks the bitterness of the poison."

Cline was released from prison in 1943 after serving 10 years of his sentence. The 60-year-old murderer quickly revived his business -- and this time he got the dosage right.

Sincerity was one of the keys to Cline's success. He presented himself as a religious and successful businessman, both of which were true. Although he regularly broke at least three of the Ten Commandments, Cline was an avid churchgoer and sang in the church choir. He was also a successful businessman, only his business was murder.

In September 1943, Cline proposed to 85- year-old Edith Lewis in Oakland, California. They honeymooned in Florida where Edith died of heart failure. Cline collected $15,000 in assets. A month later in the Sunshine State, he met Mrs. Alice Carpenter. They left for California in February 1944, but they never made it. Alice died in a Dallas hotel, leaving Cline $15,000 richer.

In May 1945, Cline struck pay dirt in the person of Mrs. Eva Krebs, a Chicago widow with a $250,000 estate. He married her and said they would take a trip to Oregon. But first they went south to Texas. Cline wrote to Eva's family, saying that Eva wanted to write them herself but had injured her hand, so she was dictating the letter to him. Since Eva never wrote her family and always communicated by phone, Cline's letter made them very suspicious. Eva's nephew hired a private detective who found that the signatures on Eva's annuity checks had been forged.

In October, Cline gave Eva Krebs a glass of buttermilk with predictable results. Cline had her cremated under someone else's name so he could continue cashing her lucrative annuity checks. But with Eva's relatives on his trail, he needed her to be legally dead so he could inherit her estate. He needed a body.

"Just think of me coming into so much good fortune," exclaimed Isabella Van Netta, a poor 73- year-old widow, to her friend Sue. "God has been so good to me. Mr. Cline seems to have so much interest in me and how he could, I don't understand."

Cline offered Van Netta a place to live and a job managing one of his apartments in Southern California. He loaded her meager belongings in his trailer, and they prepared to go south. But first, he explained, they had to make a brief stop in Portland, Oregon.

"THE LORD GIVETH AND THE LORD TAKETH AWAY" began the telegram Alfred Cline sent to Eva Krebs's nephew. AUNT EVA DIED IN PORTLAND OREGON AFTER SHORT ILLNESS. TO BE CREMATED TODAY. ASHES WILL BE INURNED AT CEMETERY IN SAN FRANCISCO."

Eva's nephew called San Francisco police and told them his suspicions. The police investigated, found the cemetery with the ashes, located Cline at the Mark Twain Hotel, and arrested him for forgery. Police found a treasure trove of evidence in Cline's room, including notebooks with over 100 names of past and future victims. Information in these notebooks led to murder investigations in Florida, Texas, Nevada, and Oregon.

The choir-singing Cline met many of his victims at church. The women, mostly elderly widows, were flattered by the attentions of a younger, prosperous, and devoutly religious man. They invited him to their houses, which he carefully inspected to determine whether they were wealthy enough to kill. It was evident that Cline was running a very successful enterprise. His safety deposit box contained $165,000 in stocks, $26,000 in cash, and a large quantity of women's jewelry.

Cline hired the legendary Jake "The Master" Erlich, the lawyer on whom Perry Mason was based. Jake's motto was "never plead guilty". The high-profile attorney had defended 56 individuals accused of murder and never allowed one to be sent to the gallows. One of the strangest trials in San Francisco history was about to begin.

Although Cline was charged with forgery, murder would play an important role in the trial. For Cline to inherit his wives' estates through forgery, he had to know that they were dead. If the DA could prove that Cline was the only person with the means, motive, and opportunity to kill these women, it would go a long way toward convicting him of forgery.

Prosecutor Norman Elkington led a parade of witnesses who put Cline at the death scenes. A witness testified that Cline was actively involved in his wife's medical care. "Coffee is not good for her. She should drink buttermilk," he told one doctor. He often told doctors that his wife was a Christian Scientist and refused to take medicine.

Using a comparison of cremation ashes, dental charts, and morticians' testimony, prosecutors proved that the body in Portland was really that of Mrs. Van Netta and that the body in Texas was really that of Eva Krebs.

The strongest witness against Cline was Clark Sellers, a noted document expert, who had testified in the famous Lindbergh kidnapping case. Sellers methodically showed the jury nine instances of forgery on the part of Cline. Eight of those instances related to the Eva Krebs case. Erlich argued that the charges should be combined into one count, but Judge Kaufman refused, and the nine counts of forgery remained.

The case suddenly hit an unexpected speed bump. Two police inspectors noticed that juror number 11 looked somewhat familiar. His juror form listed him as an interior designer, but the detectives recognized him from an earlier career as a forger. Both sides and the police met in the judge's chambers to figure a way out of this sticky situation. it turned out that juror number 11 had lied on the juror form because he was embarrassed about his past. They let him off with a $250 fine and replaced him with an alternate juror.

Then, in a move that flummoxed everyone, Alfred Cline requested a private audience with Judge Kaufman, a move without legal precedent. Up to this point, Alfred Cline had said nothing, even to Jake Ehrlich, his own lawyer. This might be the last chance to get to the bottom of the mystery that Cline had created. Judge Kaufman agreed to meet with him. They disappeared into the judge's chambers, and there they stayed for the next hour and ten minutes.

Years later, Judge Kaufman revealed the conversation to Nancy Barr Mavity, a celebrated crime writer: "Cline approached me like a salesperson, trying to sell me a lighter concurrent sentence, but never in his approach did he show the slightest feeling of horror, remorse or regret," the judge said. "But I was never cruel to them," Cline told Kaufman, giving a perfect example of the mind of a sociopath. "I bore them no ill will...I always felt quite kindly towards them and acted so," he said. Cline's sales attempt failed.

When they emerged from the judge's chambers, Kaufman announced that he had agreed to reveal nothing of the conversation. A dumbfounded Jake Ehrlich told reporters, "You can call the undertakers. I've seen everything now!" The trial continued as if the meeting had been a momentary illusion.

The case went to the jury on April 18. The jury returned an hour and a half later with a guilty verdict on nine counts of forgery. Judge Kaufman ruled that the sentences should run consecutively and gave Cline the maximum, 126 years in prison. With Cline put away for life, the murder charges, which would've been difficult to prove, were dropped.

Two years later, in a kind of irony, Cline dropped dead of a genuine, non-buttermilk related heart attack.

The House on Billionaire Street

*Bill Thoreson's mansion, at 2801 Broadway Street,
contained 79 tons of deadly weapons.
(Collection of the author, 2015)*

The 2800 block of San Francisco's Broadway Avenue, known as Billionaires' Row, is the richest block in the most expensive neighborhood of the costliest city in the United States. Prominent billionaires, such as Gordon Getty and Larry Ellison own homes on this street. In the last few years, properties at 2840 and 2845 each sold for over $32,000,000. In many ways, 2801 Broadway, a 7,000-square-foot mansion designed by noted architect Albert Fair, fits right in.

But 2801 Broadway has a sinister history that belies its tony setting. Between 1965 and 1970, this house was a massive arsenal, containing tons of machine guns and other munitions. It was the home of

William Thoresen III, a man with the face of a movie star and the mind of a serial killer.

Bill Thoresen, born in 1937, started his life with every advantage. His father was William Thoresen Jr., founder of Chicago's Great Western Steel Corporation. Thoresen built his company into one of the Midwest's largest steel-processing concerns and amassed a fortune of $70 million. Bill's mother, Kay, a former Southern belle, collected fine antiques, and the couple was well known for their philanthropic activities. The family lived in Kenilworth, Illinois, a wealthy Chicago suburb of 2,500 people.

Whoever said "money can't buy happiness" could have used Bill as Exhibit A. Even as a child, Bill had an explosive and violent temper, which was amplified by an extreme sense of entitlement, known today as "affluenza." He complained about his workaholic father and socialite mother. "They never had any time for me. I've been in military academies, boarding schools, and summer camps ever since I was nine years old. Even when I was home, they had servants to look after the house and servants to look after me and Richard," Bill complained. Thoreson spent his teenage years acting out his resentment by breaking into local homes, fighting, driving recklessly, bullying his younger brother, Richard, and warring with his parents. Bill became well known to police for his activities, but his family connections shielded him from any real consequences. He dropped out of high school.

In desperation, his parents had Bill committed to a mental institution when he was seventeen. This led to a series of escapes and recaptures until an agreement between Bill and his parents was reached. Bill would live at home and see a psychiatrist regularly. The psychiatrist would also serve a mediator between Bill and his parents. In return, his parents gave Bill a living allowance.

At twenty, Bill met Louise Banich, a twenty- one-year-old English and speech teacher from a working-class family. It was a classic case of a good girl-bad boy attraction. Bill was handsome, charismatic, and rich. Louise saw the vulnerable little boy in him. He stuttered; she was a speech therapist. She thought she could fix him. But life worked out differently. Instead of Louise bringing out the good in Bill, Bill brought out the bad in Louise. Beneath her virtuous surface was a part of her that was thrilled by his rebelliousness and by the drama that enveloped him. His psychopathic energy and charm completely dominated her.

As Bill neared his twenty-first birthday, he quit his clerk job. He had quit or been fired from every job he ever had. Thoresen didn't care because he expected to come into a large fortune when he turned 21. But that birthday came and went without any inheritance; just a birthday card on his dinner plate.

Bill and Louise went on a road trip through Canada a few months later. Bill became furious when his parents refused his request for more money, and he began shoplifting small items. When Bill and Louise crossed back into Maine, he decided to up the ante.

Family friends in Kennebunk gave Bill permission to store camping equipment in their empty barn. But the camping equipment was not his own. He filled the barn with new canoes stolen from The Old Town canoe factory. Then he added a stolen travel trailer. By this time, Louise was an active participant in the robberies. But, as usual, Bill didn't know when to stop. After successfully stealing thousands of dollars' worth of camping equipment, Bill was caught pilfering some framed pictures at a ferry terminal. They were only worth about $100. He pleaded guilty to theft and had to return all the stolen merchandise.

Returning home, Thoresen took a job as a clerk at Great Western Steel, his father's company, but he and Louise continued their shoplifting ways. Like his mother, Bill was a collector, but his accumulation was much more deadly. He convinced Louise to steal a rifle from Marshall Field's, which he added to his armament stockpile, a collection that included an illegal Thompson sub- machine gun.

Like his ordnance, Bill was a weapon waiting for the right spark to detonate. It happened in December 1959. His parents had refused to buy him a new car, and he was reduced to driving an old auto that belonged to his father's company. Bill exploded when his suit coat was stained by oil in the car. He kicked out the driver's window and grabbing a tire iron, destroyed every window in the car. He accidentally cut his Achilles tendon in the process and was taken to the hospital. His parents had him committed again to a mental institution, but he escaped and Louise picked him up.

They got married, moved to Tucson, Arizona, and had a son they named Michael. Bill reached another détente with his parents, and he and Louise lived on an allowance they sent. But Bill had not forgotten his inheritance. While visiting his parents' house, he took his father's keys, opened a vault in the basement and took a duffel bag marked with his name on it. Bill opened the duffel bag when he returned to Tucson and found $625,000 in securities his parents had been keeping from him. He also learned that parents had left a much larger sum to his younger brother.

With his new wealth, William collected a retinue of followers, including drug dealers Stoney Richardson and Cal Burlow, who joined Bill in a marijuana smuggling business.

Marriage and fatherhood never impinged on Bill's playboy lifestyle. He came and went mysteriously, drove a Ferrari, and dated stewardesses and models. But his dark side kept emerging. Bill started beating Louise. He was arrested on explosive charges and served six months in jail for sexual assault in Los Angeles. Bill was soon on a first-name basis with top criminal attorneys such as Melvin Belli.

Bill's brother, who had been living in Europe, returned to the States. Bill told Richard about the money their parents were keeping from them and convinced Richard to join him in a plan to extract more of their inheritance. They stole financial papers and embarrassed their parents with a series of wild stunts. Then they offered to return the papers in exchange for more of their inheritance. In response, their father swore out a warrant for their arrest. Bill avoided arrest by going to Hawaii and left Richard to face the music. Richard was arrested and quickly bailed out of jail. He then started his own gun collection and became depressed and paranoid.

Two days before his case came to court, on September 25, 1965, Richard was found dead in his car, with a bullet hole behind his right ear.

Because of Richard's state of mind, authorities were uncertain whether the death was suicide or homicide.

The brothers had made out wills leaving their money to each other. With the money he inherited from Richard, Bill moved to San Francisco, bought the mansion at 2801 Broadway, and discovered the pleasures of Haight-Ashbury. He hosted LSD parties at his Pacific Heights home for his Arizona friends and others.

With his customary impulsiveness, Bill decided to expand his gun collection. He and Louise traveled around the country making huge purchases of both legal and contraband arms. Mysterious crates began arriving at 2801 Broadway. But Bill did more than buy guns; he also sold them. He became an arms dealer to the Minutemen, a right-wing terrorist organization.

On September 18, 1966, the town of Kenilworth made headlines when Valerie Percy, daughter of Charles Percy, the Republican candidate for US Senate, was murdered. It was the first and only murder in Kenilworth history. She was beaten and stabbed by an intruder who had broken a window and climbed up the drainpipe into her second-story bedroom. The FBI considered Thoresen a possible suspect, but he refused to talk with them, and at the time there was no evidence linking him to the murder.

FBI and police investigators talked to thousands of people and tracked leads all across the country, but the case remains unsolved. It is considered the most famous unsolved crime in Chicago history.

On December 20, 1966, Louise Thoresen was arrested at Kennedy Airport in New York on charges of interstate shipment of explosives and illegal firearms. Authorities then raided the house at 2801 Broadway and found the largest private arsenal in US history. The weapons inside the crates included 37-millimeter cannons, anti-aircraft guns, machine guns, sub-machine guns, mortars, anti-tank rifles, grenade launchers and 668,000 rounds of ammunition. The FBI estimated that the house contained 70 tons of armaments.

Bill's defense attorney, the legendary Jake Ehrlich, characterized his client as "kind of a screwball. He just likes to collect old weapons." Bill justified his collection by saying, "I collect rocks, I collect stamps, I collect guns." He referred to the cannon as a "lawn ornament," adding, "Every lawn should have one."

Bill was furious over the police raid. He blamed his wife and began beating her regularly. Louise wore over-sized sunglasses to cover the bruises. The family moved to a house in Fresno as they fought the weapons charges in court. Over the next three years, Bill's behavior became even more erratic.

Louise tried to get him to seek psychiatric care, but he resisted. On the evening of June 9, 1970, Bill explained why. "If they use any of those truth drugs on me, they will never let me out." He then told Louise the real story of Richard's death. "It was Stoney Richardson who killed Richard. I paid him to do it." Bill later killed Richardson in the house at 2801 Broadway. Thoresen also revealed that he had tried to murder his parents and had planned to kill Louise. The next morning, he told Louise that she knew too much to live. As he got out of bed, she grabbed a gun and shot him five times, killing him instantly. Louise was arrested for murder.

At her trial, the prosecutor claimed that she shot Thoresen as he lay sleeping. The pathologist disputed this, testifying that Thoresen had a large dose of LSD in his blood at the time of his death and was probably awake. A psychiatrist described Thoresen as "a dangerous man, full of anger and hatred."

In addition, witnesses testified that Bill Thoresen:

- Tried to hire three different men to kill his wife, Louise.

- Attempted to push Louise out of a 20-story building.

- Offered a man $250,000 to kill his parents.

- Plotted to bomb Caesar's Palace in Las Vegas.

- Attacked his wife with an electric cattle prod.

- Asked a fellow inmate in San Francisco to help him commit suicide.

- Asked two different men to burn down his San Francisco mansion.

- Forced his wife to write suicide notes the night before she killed him.

Louise was acquitted on the grounds of self-defense.

But even in death, Bill Thoresen's notoriety continued. He was named as a suspect in the 1957 murder of Judith Mae Anderson, whose body was found in a barrel used in his father's factory. In 2014, he emerged as the chief suspect in the Valerie Percy murder. The murder weapon, a bayonet, was found on a beach a few days later. Bill Thoresen had hundreds of bayonets in his military collection. Footprints from the bayonet led toward Thoresen's parents' house, which was only two blocks from the Percy house. The unusual weapon used in the murder, the brutality of the attack, and the fact that nothing was taken from the house all point to Thoresen rather than a professional burglar.

In 1974, Louise wrote a book about her life with her psychopathic, serial killer of a husband, William Thoresen III. She called it "It Gave Everybody Something to Do." The title could have been worse. She wanted to call it "Sweet William."

Paul Drexler

PURVEYORS OF SIN

If San Francisco was bidding to host the Olympics of Sin, this 1876 description by Benjamin Lloyd, the author of "Lights and Shades of San Francisco," should have been part of the proposal.

"The Barbary Coast is the haunt of the low and the vile of every kind. The petty thief, the house burglar, the tramp, the whore-monger, lewd women, cutthroats, murderers, are all found here. Low gambling houses, thronged with riot-loving rowdies, in all stages of intoxication, are there. Opium dens, where heathen Chinese and God-forsaken men and women are sprawled in miscellaneous confusion, disgustingly drowsy or completely overcome, are there. Licentiousness, debauchery, pollution, loathsome disease, insanity from dissipation, misery, poverty, wealth, profanity, blasphemy, and death, are there. And Hell, yawning to receive the putrid mass, is there also."

For over seventy-five years San Francisco's Barbary Coast possessed a well-earned reputation as the most depraved and glamorous location in the United States. Jerome Bassity, Inez Burns, Bones Remmer, and Sally Stanford were the most prominent and successful purveyors of sin during San Francisco's last great era of corruption.

Paul Drexler

Jerome Bassity: King of the Tenderloin

Jerome Bassity, also known as "The King of the Tenderloin," was the face of San Francisco vice for almost 20 years. At the apex of his power, Bassity, once described by a local reporter as "a man with the moral intelligence scarcely above a trained chimpanzee," virtually controlled the San Francisco's police force.

Born into poverty in 1876, Jerome was orphaned at the age of 8. He sold newspapers by day and ushered in a theatre by night to support himself. Always a hustler, he was making $100 a month by the time he was 11. His first adult job, as a milkman, gave no sign of what he would become. He caught the eye of one of his customers, a leading Tenderloin madam, who set him up in a saloon at Golden Gate Avenue and Market Street.

Bassity took to the saloon business like an alligator takes to murky water, and he soon branched into prostitution, gambling, and narcotics. He gained stature by becoming the intermediary between the vice merchants and the corrupt city government run by Abe Reuf and Eugene Schmitz. By the early 1900s, he was the most powerful underworld figure on the Barbary Coast, owning dozens of brothels.

Bassity demonstrated his influence by opening a new brothel in 1906, despite the activities of a grand jury investigating his activities. "I don't give a snap for the grand jury," he said. "I'm going to open and they can't stop me." And he did, opening a new brothel at 1731 Commercial Street with a wild debauch in which everything was free.

The earthquake and fire destroyed much of the Barbary Coast, but sin is resilient. Within three-months of the earthquake, the brothels, bars and dance halls were back. By 1907, it was running full steam. But it was a somewhat different Barbary Coast -- just as tawdry but not as dangerous. Dance halls featured a "slummers' balcony" where well-heeled tourists could watch "authentic Barbary Coast life" while they bought overpriced drinks.

Bassity extended his reach into the Tenderloin when he bought the Coronado Saloon on Mason and Ellis streets in 1907. Saloonkeepers in the area were delighted because they knew that where Jerome went, prostitution and gambling were sure to follow.

Because Bassity was a vice lord, a drug dealer, a drunkard, and a corrupter, his historical reputation is largely negative. But there is one area, popular culture, in which Bassity deserves some credit. Red light districts provide a cross-fertilization of cultures and opportunity and freedom to artists. Irish clog dancing met African dancing in New York City's Five Points slum in the 1820s, a union that produced tap dancing.

By the late 19th century, the Barbary Coast's energy and dynamism were already attracting luminaries such as Oscar Wilde and Sarah Bernhardt. San Francisco's musical influence began when George Walker and Bert Williams, who were to become the greatest African American stars in vaudeville history, met in San Francisco in 1893. Walker and Williams took the cakewalk -- a dance slaves had competed in -- and put their spin on it. The two men brought it to New York, where it became an enormous hit and was adopted by the white middle and upper class. Bassity provided the political cover and protection that allowed this music to flourish. He even served as a judge at some of the cakewalk contests.

The 500 block of Pacific Street was the epicenter of new trends in music. On this block were the Thalia, the biggest dance hall on the West Coast, and Purcell's So Different Club, one of the few integrated nightclubs in the country. It was at this club where New Orleans Jazz was first heard on the West Coast, and many of the dance crazes of the early 20th Century, like the Texas Tommy and the Turkey Trot, all started there. Next to Purcell's was Spider Kelly's, which installed sheet metal in the wall behind the bar to protect the bartenders from the result of armed arguments happening in Purcell's.

Famous vaudeville entertainers like Al Jolson and Sophie Tucker came to Pacific Street as young performers. They took what they learned and spread it to the rest of the country. The great Russian dancer, Anna Pavlova, often visited here and said she learned many dance moves that she later added to her own repertoire.

Bassity's rackets brought him around $8,000 a month, and he was a firm believer in the "if you got it flaunt it" philosophy. He wore three diamond rings on each hand, a huge gem on his shirtfront, and over fifty custom-made, embroidered waistcoats. He spent enormous sums on jewelry, most of which went to prostitutes at his competitors' brothels. But despite his heavy spending, he was rarely a welcome guest due to his behavior. Bassity was always armed, drank heavily, and often ended an evening by shooting out the lights in the brothel. He was arrested twice for shooting at people on the street.

In the early morning of February 8, 1908, a drunken Bassity began yelling and looking for trouble in a restaurant located in a building that he owned. Trouble, in the form of an angry waiter and cook, found him. When police arrived, "Bassity looked as though he had fought a battle with a wildcat and received decidedly the worst of the battle." Officers took him to the hospital and then sent him to jail for disturbing the peace. On a previous occasion, Bassity visited the same restaurant around the same time in the morning and fired several shots through the floor and ceiling because he contended "the people about the place wasted too much electricity."

The reform movement temporarily closed Bassity's places, but he saw his chance when Patrick McCarthy ran for mayor in 1910. As the manager of McCarthy's non-political Liberty League, Bassity raised huge sums for his campaign. McCarthy promised to "make San Francisco the Paris of the West," and Jerome was just the man to help put the sin back in San Francisco. In an article, titled "Underworld Czar for McCarthy," the San Francisco Call described McCarthy's supporters as "the keepers of every deadfall and dive in San Francisco. The beasts who live off the shame of fallen women." When McCarthy won, Bassity became part of a triumvirate who controlled the police force.

He got his friend Dan White appointed police chief. Bassity then brought all the corrupt police back to the Tenderloin and sent honest policemen like Arthur Layne (great-grandfather of Governor Jerry Brown) to the outlying districts. Gambling and prostitution flourished, and "Bunko Men" trolled the Ferry Building to lure the unwary to Bassity-owned clubs. When a police commissioner crony was tried for corruption, Jerome sent three call girls to influence men on the jury.

Bassity's power began to fade when "Sunny Jim" Rolfe was elected mayor in 1912. The years of high living were showing as his double chins began to multiply and his pants expanded annually. But though his body enlarged, his common sense remained tiny.

He started a bar fight with an Alaskan fisherman who pounded him like a fat piece of abalone. Bassity threatened reprisals but didn't follow through, and he lost his stature in the underworld. By 1917, Bassity's influence was gone, and he was arrested for serving a soldier in his saloon. How far the mighty had fallen.

The rest of his life was anticlimactic. He sold his interests in San Francisco, moved to Southern California, and spent most of his resources in a failed attempt to buy a Tijuana racetrack. When he died in San Diego in 1929, he left an estate of less than $10,000. But in his heyday, Jerome Bassity took great pride in being the most popular answer to the question, "Who is the wickedest man in San Francisco?"

A Necessary Evil

San Francisco's most famous abortionist knew how to trim a cuticle, but that was the extent of her medical training. Born Inez Brown to a poor family in San Francisco's South of the Slot neighborhood in 1886, she became a manicurist in the Palace hotel at the age of 17. With her good looks and outgoing personality, she soon became a customer favorite. One of her customers was Dr. Eugene West, a notorious abortionist who had been acquitted of murder in the 1893 death of Addie Gilmore.

In those days, most abortions were done in a doctor's office and the woman was sent home on the same day. If complications occurred, women rarely went to the hospital, either because the doctor was afraid of losing his license or because the patient was afraid of losing her reputation. As a result, thousands of women died needlessly each year.

Dr. West saw something in Inez, and he hired her as a receptionist for his clinic. Over time, she became quite skilled in performing the operation, becoming so proficient that she took over the business when Dr. West retired. By 1922, she had made enough money to buy and outfit a three-story building at 327 Fillmore Street.

Patient safety was one of Inez's top priorities, and she designed her Fillmore Street offices like a modern hospital ward. She outfitted multiple rooms with beds for recovering patients, and her operating room was spotless and furnished with the latest surgical instruments and equipment. She hired a staff of registered nurses, a blood technician, and others to provide professional care. She also installed trap doors to escape through, in the event of a police raid.

As her reputation spread, so did her practice, especially among the well connected. Her patients included socialites, politicians' wives, prostitutes, even movie stars like Rita Hayworth and Sonja Henie. She performed up to 30 abortions a week, charging $75 to $200, though she sometimes provided her services gratis to poor women. During her best years, Inez grossed $50,000 a month, the equivalent of more than $600,000 in today's money.

The home she built at 274 Guerrero Street in the city's Mission District was outfitted with the finest furniture and materials. Because her business was illegal, Inez couldn't use banks. Instead, she built secret compartments to store the vast amount of cash flowing into her coffers. This proved to be an expensive mistake when termites ate $750,000 hidden in her wine cellar. In 1932, Inez married her fourth husband, Joseph Burns, a California Assemblyman, and took his last name.

They bought a 1,000-acre ranch in La Honda where they raised and trained racehorses.

For almost 25 years, the business was woven into the fabric of San Francisco and protected by bonds of friendship, fear, greed, and respect. The friendship was for her husband, Joe, whose Wednesday night poker game included many high-ranking cops who were childhood friends. The fear was that of her prominent business and society clients who feared exposure if she went to court. As to the greed, police and politicians accepted her bribes in return for warning her of impending police raids. And the respect was from her clients and others who appreciated her unmatched safety record.

Her Fillmore Street clinic was raided in 1936 and 1938, but she was never charged because no one would testify against her. She settled an income tax evasion charge in 1939 by paying a $10,000 fine. But her luck changed in 1943 when Pat Brown, an ambitious young district attorney, was elected on an anti-corruption platform. On September 26, 1945, police raided the clinic only to find that Inez had escaped a few minutes before in her limousine. Police Inspector Frank Ahearn raced over to Inez's Guerrero Street home and discovered a safe containing $289,000. She offered Frank the money not to arrest her, but he turned her down immediately. This established Ahearn's reputation for incorruptibility, which helped him become the SFPD chief of police.

Ahearn also seized a handful of notebooks with names, dates and dollar amounts, indicating that Burns had performed $500,000 worth of abortions in 1944. DA Brown reported this to the IRS and indicted Burns. The grand jury again refused to indict her, citing insufficient evidence. Undaunted, Brown continued building his case and re-arrested Inez on October 27, 1945. His revelation that prominent people might be named in the case made it front page news. Police also announced that they were seeking Lavina Queen, Burn's anesthetist, who had escaped the police raid.

Inez was indicted and the case went to trial. Prosecutor Tom Lynch was well prepared. He called thirty witnesses, including two former employees, three former clients, medical suppliers, and police. Lynch presented fifty-nine exhibits, including a hospital bed, tanks of nitrous oxide and oxygen, trays of medical instruments, and patient records. Confidently, the prosecution rested; it was the defense's turn. After a pregnant pause, Walter McGovern, Inez's attorney, slowly stood up and said: "In view of the total insufficiency of evidence, Your Honor, we rest too."

The courtroom was stunned. The court recessed for the day. McGovern turned to the baffled crowd and said: "Wait for tomorrow."

McGovern's summary to the jury the next day introduced a startling new defendant: the district attorney. "Don't make these defendants the goat on the sacrificial altar of the political ambitions of Pat Brown," McGovern thundered, referring to Brown's campaign to be California's attorney general. McGovern argued that Inez had been providing a necessary, albeit illegal, service for over 20 years. It was a service that the public understood and permitted. The only reason she was being prosecuted at this time was to build Brown's reputation for the political campaign, McGovern claimed.

He was asking the jury to disregard the law and vote their common sense. The jury deliberated for fifteen hours and was deadlocked after eighty- five ballots, voting eleven to one to convict. A mistrial was declared. Asecond trial also ended in a hung jury. But in the third trial, in 1946, with Lavina Queen, Burn's anesthetist testifying under immunity, and a prosecution friendly judge, Inez and her co-defendants were convicted. They were sentenced to 2 to 5 years each.

It was not just Pat Brown's ambitions that ended Inez's career. The heavily Irish Catholic police and court system regarded abortion as a mortal sin. The public opinion pendulum of San Francisco was swinging from open town to a respectable city, and the male establishment wanted women out of the offices and factories and back in the kitchens.

Burns was released after two years, but her troubles were far from over. She was convicted of tax evasion and for performing another abortion, and she spent another 14 months in jail. In 1956, she was forced to pay more than $740,000 in back taxes to the IRS, which wiped out the rest of her fortune. Inez and Joe Burns spent their final years in a nursing home in Moss Beach. She died in 1976 at the age of 87.

Late in life, Pat Brown, who served two terms as California's governor, was asked about Inez Burns. "She was a very good abortionist with a good reputation. Everyone thought she was a necessary evil. But when I became D.A., her business had become flagrant."

Bones Remmer

Anyone with the belief that fat people are jolly never met Elmer "Bones" Remmer, San Francisco's one- time gambling czar. Casino owner Warren Nelson, who worked for Remmer, described Bones as "the meanest, crudest guy who ever lived." For a man like this, a name like Elmer does not seem to fit. The name Bones, however, seemed oddly appropriate for Renner, who weighed over 300 pounds.

Remmer was hired in 1929 to manage Lake Tahoe's Cal Neva Lodge, one of Nevada's oldest casinos, by owners Bill Graham and Jim McKay. The next year, Remmer made headlines when he tried unsuccessfully to collect a $13,000 blackjack debt run up by Clara Bow, a movie star known as "The It Girl."

Bones was a large, tough man with an appetite for both power and food. As time passed, both his waistline and his ownership in the Lodge increased. He took over the club when Graham and McKay were sent to jail for mail fraud in 1937.

The Cal Neva Lodge had a profitable sideline: laundering money for racketeers and bank robbers. Remmer cleaned "hot" bank robbery money for desperados like Alvin Karpis and Baby Face Nelson. Remmer let Nelson hide out in cabins near the lodge and introduced him to California bootleggers, who hired Baby Face to protect their liquor shipments. Nelson returned the favor by killing an important witness against Graham and McKay and burying him in the desert. By this time, Remmer had a well-earned reputation for collecting gambling debts. "Listen," he told a reluctant debtor at his Tahoe casino, "It's a big lake and it ain't full yet, if you know what I mean. You're going to pay this off, and I mean now!" He got his money.

As big city organized crime became more sophisticated, it looked for ways to protect itself from the occasional reform administration. One way was to take over a nearby small city and move vice operations there. In the 1920s, the Chicago mob, under Al Capone, took over Cicero, Illinois. In the late 1930s, Remmer, under Lucky Luciano and Bugsy Siegel, took over Emeryville, a small industrial town between Oakland and San Francisco. Governor Earl Warren called Emeryville "the rottenest city on the Pacific Coast." It was Remmer who put the "rot" in "rotten," running the town from the Townhouse, a windowless saloon, while John Bauters, his handpicked mayor, drank at the bar. He ran the Oaks Room Card Club, which is still in operation, as well as a number of brothels in the city. He was also involved with importing and selling narcotics.

Remmer also ran the 21 Club in El Cerrito, as well as the 110 Eddy and the Menlo Club in San Francisco. It is said that Pat Brown, in the days before he became a DA, did the legal work in incorporating the Menlo Club. Bones, an oversized man with a personality to match, became a well- known San Francisco character. Legendary gamblers like Nick the Greek and Ty Thompson (the inspiration for Damon Runyan's Sky Masterson) played for high stakes at the Menlo Club. Jack Ruby, Lee Harvey Oswald's assassin, also worked at the club in the 1940s, along with his sisters Eva and Ruby, who were card dealers.

Money poured into the Remmer coffers. But as the Bob Dylan song says, "You've got to serve somebody." For Remmer, it was definitely not the Lord, it was organized crime. Much of his gambling profits went to higher-ups; gangsters such as Lucky Luciano, Bugsy Siegel, and San Francisco Mafia boss Jimmy Lanza. When Siegel was assassinated in 1947, many people thought Remmer would be next. But Bones was a survivor.

Remmer spread his largesse liberally among state and local politicians. Local police and DAs usually overlooked his activities in their town. He had numerous fronts for his gambling operations. You couldn't get a cigar at Remmer's B&R Smokeshop at 50 Mason Street, but you could always make a bet on the horses.

Remmer also gave $170,000 in campaign contributions to California Attorney General Fred Howser to look the other way. So, Bones was irked in April 1948 when San Francisco's DA Pat Brown raided The Menlo Club and arrested 100 gamblers and 14 club employees. After two trials that ended in hung juries, Remmer went free.

Remmer, along with St. Louis bookie Tommy Walen and Hollywood actress Vici Raaf, was arrested in LA in 1950 after a nightclub brawl. Bones was subpoenaed to testify about gambling by the Kefauver Senate Crime Commission, but he managed to hide in Mexico until the hearings were over.

Some of the material discovered in the hearings led to a most unusual lawsuit. During the hearings, SFPD Homicide Chief Frank Ahearn revealed that police had recordings of Southern California mobsters discussing the possibility of killing Remmer. On April 25, 1950, Remmer filed a damage suit against Ahearn, claiming that Ahearn neglected his duty "to watch over the safety of citizens from assault, destruction, and injury and prevent the commission of crimes." Remmer asked for damages of $5,000 multiplied by the number of people involved in the plot. Remmer also demanded that Ahearn reveal all information involved in the recordings. The lawsuit went nowhere.

Although Remmer was able to beat local gambling charges he could not avoid one of the two certainties in life: taxes. The IRS seized his assets, charged him with tax evasion, and he was convicted in 1952 of evading over $128,000 in taxes. During one of his arrests, he was heard to give the classic protest spoken by well-to-do felons: "You can't do this to me. I've got money." He won a new trial on appeal but was convicted again in 1956 and served two-and-a-half years. In 1959 the government sold Remmer's assets, collecting $863,000 in fines and taxes. Bones spent his last days bemoaning his losses, reminiscing about the good old days, and selling cars on his brother's car lot. He died in 1963 at the age of 65.

Paul Drexler

Sally Stanford From Madam to Mayor

*Sally Stanford had 8 marriages, 17 arrests,
28 aliases, and $20 million.
(SF Library History Room, 1945)*

When it comes to reinventing yourself, Sally Stanford was in a class by herself. She was born Mabel Busby in Oregon. Her mother was a teacher; her father, an alcoholic who died at an early age. Sally was an entrepreneur from the very beginning. At the age of seven, she convinced golfers at the local golf course to let her work as their caddy.

At 16, she eloped with Dan Gooden, who had embezzled $5,000 from a lumber mill, and began her collection of husbands (8), and names (over 30). Knowing nothing of Gooden's crime, Sally cashed a $10 check on the embezzled funds and was later arrested. She was sentenced to two years for this heinous crime in July 1920. While in prison, Sally learned how to get into bootlegging -- and she learned well. After her release in 1921, she opened up a speakeasy in Ventura, California. She stimulated sales by serving salty roasted chicken.

In 1923, she married criminal attorney Ernest Spignoli and moved to San Francisco. The next year, she took her bootlegging profits, bought a hotel at 695 O'Farrell Street in San Francisco's Tenderloin district, and moved from bootlegging to brothels. Under police pressure, Sally moved to 676 Geary, then 750 Taylor, expanding her business as she traveled. She was arrested 17 times but was convicted only twice, paying fines of

$250 each time. She used the name Sally Stanford during one of her arrests after seeing an article about the Stanford football team, and the name stuck. She claimed to have never paid the police for protection during her bordello years. Of course, it helped to have friends like Mayor Jim Rolph, who was often a guest in her establishment. Her last two sporting houses were designed like fortresses. By the time police could batter their way through two sturdy doors, her guests and girls had exited via a secret staircase and all evidence of prostitution was gone.

Sally was the white whale in Police Sergeant John Dyer's version of Moby Dick. Dyer played the role of Captain Ahab for over twenty years as he obsessively pursued Sally. He sent plain-clothed vice cops posing as wealthy clubmen and salesmen to try to get inside Sally's house. He even climbed up a wall and tried to sneak onto her roof. He was never successful. Dyer retired early and obtained a disability pension, claiming his pursuit of Sally had caused a heart attack.

In 1940, she bought a mansion reportedly designed by Stanford White at 1044 Pine Street, which became the most famous bordello in the country. The architectural highlight was a majestic Pompeian Court with a huge fountain and fireplace. In the corner of the court was a nine-foot marble bath in which Broadway star Anna Held used to take milk baths. Sally's girls were the prettiest and most elegantly gowned; her place the most sumptuous. The most powerful politicians, businessmen, and actors flocked to her establishment. Errol Flynn and Frank Sinatra were regular customers. But Sally had strict standards of behavior at her place. She once threw Humphrey Bogart out of her house for being drunk and obnoxious.

She may even have played a role in establishing world peace. San Francisco Chronicle Columnist Herb Caen claimed that the United Nations was founded at her bordello because many of the delegates attending the founding conference in June 1945 were her customers, and a large part of the actual negotiations took place in her living room.

Sally once listed the characteristics of a successful madam: "courage, an infinite capacity for perpetual suspicion, stamina on a 24-hour basis, the deathless conviction that the customer is always wrong, a fair knowledge of first and second aid, do-it-yourself gynecology, judo, and a tremendous sense of humor".

She demonstrated these characteristics in 1947 when Mark Monroe and Thomas Sitler, two armed thugs, broke into her house at 1977 Clay Street. She woke up to find the two men pointing guns at her face. "Give us the keys to your closet or we'll kill you." "Go ahead and shoot me," Sally yelled as the men started pistol-whipping her. "With me dead, you'll get nothing but the chair." With blood pouring down her face, she pushed the guns away, ran to the window and started screaming. The men fled down the stairs and were later captured and sentenced to long prison terms.

District Attorney and future governor Pat Brown raided her house in 1949, and she closed her business. Sally took her money and opened Valhalla, a successful restaurant in Sausalito. She decided to get into local politics when the Sausalito city government turned down her request to erect a restaurant sign. She was defeated in her first five attempts but was unfazed. "We sinners don't give up," she declared. She won on her sixth attempt and was eventually elected mayor.

A mercurial boss, Sally fired and rehired her staff on a regular basis, showing affection only for her parrot, Loretta, and Bessie, her Persian cat. Sally was a woman of impulsive charity. She often picked up the check for soldiers who ate at her restaurant. She would read of the death of a homeless man and anonymously pay for his funeral. She would send money in unmarked envelopes to disaster victims and contributed generously to various charities. She once said "Madaming is the sort of thing that happens to you—

like getting a battlefield commission or becoming the dean of women at Stanford University."

She died in 1982.

Quite a career path our Sally had. From Bootlegger to madam to mayor. I'd like to close with another quotation from Sally about San Francisco:

"They were a wonderful set of burglars the people who were running San Francisco when I first came to town in 1923, wonderful because if they were stealing, they were doing it with class and style."

CON ARTISTS

Con artists are performers with larceny in their souls. They fascinate us with their ability to manipulate people, their colossal nerve and imagination, and their utter lack of scruples. Some of San Francisco's most imaginative and fascinating con artists have shown themselves to be masters of illusion, turning a 300-pound woman into a femme fatale, an Australian criminal into a royal physician, and a box of random wires into a powerful medical device said to diagnose and cure almost every disease.

Whether posing as successful miners, a prosperous widow looking for matrimony, or as aristocratic physicians, they have separated us from our money with great aplomb.

Paul Drexler

The Confidence Queen

Big Bertha

*"She has the reputation of being one of the smartest
confidence women in America."
—Inspector Thomas Byrnes, NYPD
("Professional Criminals of America"
Thomas Byrnes, 1886)*

The term Big Bertha is used to describe spectacular pieces of equipment. In World War I, Big Bertha was the name given the enormous cannon used by the Germans to destroy previously impregnable forts. Today Big Bertha is used to describe the world's largest earth moving machine, capable of boring a hole 58 feet in diameter. But in the 19th century, Big Bertha described a person; a spectacular woman capable of separating previously impregnable men from their money.

In February 1888, Bertha Stanley visited Dr. Messing, chief rabbi of Beth Israel Congregation, accompanied by her stepson, Willie. She told the rabbi she had inherited $300,000 ($6,000,000 in today's money) from her husband, a Christian, but she wanted her next marriage to be with someone Jewish, her original faith. She offered $1,000 to the person who would find her a thoroughly acceptable Jewish husband. She visited Dr. Messing frequently and met Dr. Messing's brother-in-law, Abraham Gruhn, a wealthy businessman. Though the newspapers made sport of her weight, -- describing her as elephantine, comparing her to a battleship and decidedly ugly -- what she lacked in looks she made up with charisma. Gruhn fell madly in love with her and proposed marriage within a few days. There were many others to follow.

Bertha soon charmed her way into the top social class of Beth Israel, giving a check for $1,000 for the congregation and hinting at much more to come. She was the guest of honor at numerous soirées and managed to acquire an extensive wardrobe including jewelry, some as gifts, some on credit.

She told Gruhn that her son, Willie, was opposed to the marriage, and he lent Willie $500 as a way to soften his resistance. Then Bertha and Willie departed to Los Angeles, pausing only to pawn the more expensive jewels.

When Bertha's check bounced, Gruhn became suspicious and visited Captain of Detectives Isaiah Lees. Upon hearing Bertha's description, Lees reached for a book, turned to photograph #122 and showed it to Gruhn. "Is this the woman?" he inquired. A shocked Gruhn nodded his assent. The book was "Professional Criminals of America" by New York City Chief of Detectives, Thomas Byrnes.

The description read BERTHA HEYMAN, alias BIG BERTHA, CONFIDENCE QUEEN. The book, written in 1886, detailed her many swindles and noted that she was currently incarcerated, adding, "Her sentence will expire in April 1887."

"She has the reputation of being one of the smartest confidence women in America," Byrnes wrote admiringly. "She possesses a wonderful knowledge of human nature and can deceive those who consider themselves particularly shrewd in business matters," he added.

A warrant for her arrest was issued. Bertha and Willie fled Los Angeles but were captured in Texas and returned to San Francisco. With calm confidence, she was the picture of outraged innocence and soon became a press favorite. Impresario Ned Foster saw an opportunity and launched Bertha into a theatrical career after bailing her out of jail. He booked her into Woodward's Garden, and 18,000 people streamed in to see her and hear her paint herself as the victim in her poem "The Confidence Queen".

"So when vain grasping men
pant for glittering gold,
And find their bonanza in me
Is it wicked to show up how badly
they're sold, And the rogues that
men can sometimes be"

She was acquitted in the trial, though Willie was convicted and sent up to San Quentin for a short stretch.

Bertha was a guaranteed draw in whatever role she was given to play. On July 8, 1888, before a crowd of twelve hundred, she was a competitor in a remarkable spectacle at the Bay District Race Track. Tipping the scales at 300 pounds, wearing a Roman toga, a winged helmet, and brandishing a whip, Bertha competed against Miss Claude Lee, a woman of similar stature in a chariot race.

Their chariots were pulled by horses from the trolley lines that were unaccustomed to a different route. There were frequent delays as spectators and track officials struggled to point the confused horses in the direction of the finish line. Bertha, as could be expected, was the winner.

Bertha's career continued with a booking in The Bella Union, San Francisco's most popular music hall, and she discovered that her lack of talent was no barrier to popularity. She was paired with Oofty Goofty, a Barbary Coast character who made his living as a human punching bag. They staged boxing matches on stage during which she would invariably knock him out. Then, in a stroke of comic genius, Foster cast them as the title characters in Shakespeare's Romeo and Juliet. Due to Bertha's weight, the tender love scene had to played with Oofty in the balcony and Bertha on the ground.

One day she confided to her manager, Ned, that her suitcase had a false bottom, containing $10,000 in Canadian bonds and thousands of dollars in jewelry and asked him to handle the sale for her. While they negotiated over the next few days, Bertha borrowed small sums of money from him. He agreed to pay her $1,600 for the trunk, but before doing so, he snuck into her room and discovered that the false bottom was a fake.

Reporters learned of a less appealing side of Bertha in 1889 when they interviewed her first husband, Frederick Kerkow. He recalled that he met Bertha in 1869 when she was young and working for one of her relatives as a maid. Kerkow, then a banker, fell in love with Bertha and married her. Several years later, he learned she was cheating on him with a number of men and divorced her.

Bertha was born Bertha Schlessinger in 1851 in Germany. Her father spent five years in prison for check forging.

In 1890, Bertha appeared as a professional wrestler in San Francisco.

In 1893, Bertha was sued by a doctor in Spokane for alienating his wife's affections.

"The moment I discover a man's a fool, I let him drop, but I delight in getting into the confidence and pockets of men who think they can't be 'skinned,'" Bertha once said. "It ministers to my intellectual pride."

Bertha claimed not to care about the money she made and said she gave some away to needy people. The record shows otherwise. Like most con artists, Bertha robbed from everyone and kept everything.

Paul Drexler

The Great Diamond Hoax

Asbury Harpending. Was he the brains behind the Diamond Hoax? ("The Great Diamond Hoax." Asbury Harpending, 1916)

It was the greatest con in California history, brilliantly conceived and executed. No widows and orphans were created in the making of this crime. No one lost their life savings. Only the mighty were brought low.

The Hook

One night in late 1870, Phillip Arnold and his cousin, John Slack, two weather-beaten miners from Kentucky, showed up in the office of George Roberts, a prominent businessman. They were clutching an old leather bag. Inside the bag, they explained, was something of great value, which they would have deposited in the Bank of California, except for the late hour. After questioning, they reluctantly revealed that the sack contained rough diamonds, but refused to say anything else about the find. They made Roberts swear an oath of silence about the diamonds until they could explore their claim more thoroughly.

Roberts broke his promise the next day when he excitedly told his friend, William Ralston, president of the Bank of California, about the discovery. After examining the diamonds, Ralston offered to buy the miners' claim, but Arnold and his partner agreed only to sell a small part of the claim for $100,000 -- $50,000 up front and another $50,000 when the deal was complete. For collateral, the miners gave an additional sack of diamonds, which a local jeweler certified as extremely valuable. The miners left with the money and promised to return with "a couple of million dollars of stones."

Word of a fabulous treasure was starting to spread. At this point, Ralston contacted his friend, Asbury Harpending, who was in London, and asked him to take charge of the new enterprise.

Harpending's life was even more interesting than his name. Born in Kentucky in 1839, Harpending made his first fortune mining in California. During the Civil War, he joined a Southern conspiracy aimed at pirating ships carrying gold to the US Mint and taking them to the Confederacy. He was caught and served a brief jail sentence.

After the war, Harpending made another fortune in railroads and in the stock market. He was in London selling shares in a silver mine when Ralston's telegram reached him. He returned to the US just in time to meet Arnold and Slack in Reno. They had returned from another trip to the mine with a large bag containing gems, worth $1,000,000 – or so they claimed.

Harpending took the bag and went to his house where he poured the contents of the bag onto his billiard table while Ralston and other investors watched. Diamonds and other precious gems poured onto the table in front of the dazzled observers.

Harpending's next step was to have Tiffany's in New York evaluate 10% of the stones. Charles Tiffany checked out the stones himself and had his gem cutter (or lapidary) examine them. Tiffany estimated their value at $150,000, making the total find worth $1.5 million.

Matters moved quickly after that. Arnold and Slack were called in and told that they lacked the resources to develop the claim. After some debate, they settled on selling 75% of the enterprise for $600,000 (worth $11.5 million today). Arnold received $100,000 in advance and plans were made for six people, including mining expert Henry Janin, to visit the diamond fields when the winter was over.

In June 1872, Arnold and Slack led Janin and his party on a zigzag course to the diamond fields so that the precise location would not be revealed until the papers were signed. The party finally arrived at 4:00 in the afternoon. Arnold gave them advice on how to look for the stones. Within a few minutes, the men started finding diamonds in the ground, along with rubies, emeralds, and sapphires. Janin was very enthusiastic about the find and asked to buy shares in the mine.

The Payoff

Janin's enthusiastic report clinched the deal, and Arnold and Slack received their $600,000. Arnold sold his remaining shares in the mines to Harpending for an additional $200,000.

The San Francisco and New York Mining Company was formed with a Who's Who list of partners, including England's Baron Rothschild and General George McClellan. Twenty-five friends of the Ralston Group were allowed to buy stock for $80,000 each, and they were deluged with offers to sell their shares at a huge profit.

The Scam Revealed

A chance meeting on an Oakland-bound train revealed the fraud.

Members of the US Geological Survey ran into Henry Janin and learned that he may have found diamonds somewhere in the northeast corner of Colorado. This concerned them because they had surveyed that area, and if a large diamond discovery had been made, it would call into question the thoroughness of their work and threaten their agency's annual funding.

They contacted their boss, Clarence King, a Yale-educated geologist and noted explorer. King and his men left immediately to look for Janin's diamond fields. Their knowledge of the area gave them a good idea where the fields might be.

After a bitterly cold 150-mile trip, they started looking around. Around 4:00 in the afternoon, they came across a claim notice posted by Janin and started digging at the site. They found diamonds, rubies, and other precious stones and went to sleep dreaming of untold millions.

In the morning, King noticed something suspicious. He saw diamonds and rubies together even though they are not usually located in the same area. He recognized that some of the diamonds were of a type native to South Africa and that all the gems were found just one or two feet under the surface, a distribution that never occurs in nature. He even found a diamond that had been cut by a lapidary. King contacted William

Ralston immediately who reimbursed investors out of his own pocket.

A detective agency found that Arnold had bought industrial grade diamonds three times in London and Amsterdam in 1870 and 1871. He spent $8,000 initially to salt the diamond field. He returned twice and bought another $40,000 worth out of the $150,000 advances he had received from Ralston and the other investors.

The newspapers had a good time making fun of the swindled captains of industry. But it was hard to say what the investors did wrong. They had the diamonds checked out by Charles Tiffany, the leading jeweler in the country. But Tiffany was an expert in finished or cut stones. He did not have experience with rough stones.

The investors had Henry Janin, one of the leading mining experts in the country, check out the mine. However, Janin was an expert in gold and silver mining. He knew little about the geology and mining of precious stones.

Arnold and Slack had baited the hook masterfully. They swore George Roberts to secrecy, knowing he couldn't keep a secret, and pretended to be reluctant to sell their mine. They guessed that the American jewelry and mining experts would not have experience with the mining and evaluation of raw gems. They dramatically increased the size of the payoff by buying more gems with the investors' money.

The miners were long gone by the time the con was discovered. Slack had disappeared and Arnold had moved back to Kentucky where he had purchased a substantial house and land. He was indicted in San

Francisco, and when an attorney from California arrived for an extradition hearing, Arnold declared, "I have employed counsel myself —a good Henry rifle."

As Arnold accused the big California bankers of trying to cheat him, his Kentucky friends closed ranks around him. The bank's attorney, realizing the futility of winning a case in Kentucky, accepted a $150,000 settlement. When Arnold died of pneumonia six years later, more than $200,000 was missing from his estate.

Some suspected that Harpending might have been involved, but he always denied it. In 1916, Harpending wrote "The Great Diamond Hoax," which has become the standard text on the case. But he might have left something out.

"Oh, the diamonds shine bright on my own Kentucky home."

Harpending was indicted in 1874 for fraud for selling shares in the Burro silver mine. It was alleged that the rich silver ore samples from the this mine actually came from another mine. The San Francisco Chronicle also mentioned the name of Phillip Arnold in connection with this case and reported that Harpending was staying at an undisclosed location in Kentucky.

Harpending's involvement in the con also helps to explain why Arnold and Slack were perfectly willing to have experts examine the gems. Harpending was leading the investigation.

In 1944, some of Harpending's old correspondence came to light. One of the letters, written in 1871 by a close friend, refers to a Mr. Arnold of Kentucky and asks, "Can you send me one of the African rough diamonds?"

Take a look at the photo of Harpending. I think I see a $200,000 twinkle in his eye.

The Man of 1000 Aliases

*"Give me a clean shirt and a shave and I can win
the affection of any woman in the world."
—Andrew John Gibson
(California State archives, 1906)*

*"What's in a name? that which we call a rose by
any other name would smell as sweet."*

Andrew John Gibson would have disagreed with
Juliet. Then he would have seduced her, written Lord
Capulet a bad check, and moved to Denmark to borrow
money from Ophelia's father, Polonius.

For Gibson, an impressive name was an
occupational necessity. Andrew John Gibson, AKA Sir
Harry Westwood Cooper, AKA Surgeon Major Home,
V.C, AKA Dr. Milton Abraham, AKA Ebenezer McKay,
et al. was a most industrious con man. With a regal
presence and forged documents, he cut a swath of

larceny on four continents, leaving a trail of counterfeit checks and at least 12 swindled wives.

Born in Australia in 1868, Gibson was adopted by a couple who gave him the name Earnest Charles Chadwick and moved to England. Returning to Australia, he posed as the heir to a large British fortune and married the daughter of a wealthy businessman in Sydney. He left her after cashing some worthless checks and married a girl in Brisbane. Gibson took his new wife to London, where he abandoned her. Moving on to Toronto, he became Dr. Harry Westwood Cooper and used forged newspaper clipping to attest to his miraculous surgical techniques.

Thus armed, Gibson practiced medicine while delivering an occasional sermon in the Presbyterian Church. Gibson ingratiated himself with his soon-to-be-fleeced flock by pretending to be very ill and showing people the generous bequests they would receive from his huge estate.

Gibson disappeared after borrowing large sums of money and arrived in San Francisco in 1897 as Sir Harry Westwood, MD, having been knighted by the Queen of his Imagination. He was arrested there after forging a check on the Crocker Woolworth Bank and served three years in San Quentin. While in San Quentin, he initiated a plan to murder the night guards and escape. But he then betrayed his co-conspirators to win favor with the warden.

Upon his release, he became Dr. Milton Abraham and repeated the following recipe for deception: Take one impressive title, add an aristocratic attitude, marinate in forged documents. Stir thoroughly. Pour mixture over a young heiress, add money borrowed under empty promises, turn up the heat, remove the money, and disappear.

Unfortunately for Gibson, the disappearing part was flawed, and he was arrested again. Even prison could not impair his connubial criminality. He seduced Teressa Van Veldon, a wealthy Salvation Army missionary, who visited the prison, and married her under the nose of his San Francisco jailers. He promised he would reform, and she used her influence with the parole board to get him out. He soon abandoned her and fled the country.

Gibson was so persuasive that jailers were ordered not to talk with him, lest they fall under his spell. He once said, "Give me a shave and a clean shirt and I can win the affection of any woman in the world."

In 1910, Gibson courted two society debutantes, Anna Milbraith and Daisy Clemm, while he was living with a third woman in Oakland. On the same day he married Anna, he proposed to Daisy. He fled to London when the marriage was exposed.

Newspaper coverage was split between condemnation of his crimes and admiration for his wooing ability. On March 24, 1912, the San Francisco Call devoted an entire page to Gibson with the title: "Why are the Sir Harry Westwood Coopers able to find so many wives?" The three choices were: Hypnotism, Personal Charm, and Lack of Opportunities. The person who mailed in the cleverest answer would win two pieces of silverware. One answer, credited to Sir Harry's barber and tailor, won a silver pie knife. The San Francisco Chronicle's Helen Dare was unimpressed. She disdainfully described Cooper as "a common specimen of the warped, undernourished, nondescript cockney.... the sight of whom makes the sophisticated man involuntarily button his coat over his pockets and feel for his hatpin and the traveled woman take a firmer clutch of her handbag as she gives him a wide berth."

After leaving San Francisco, Gibson continued his career abroad. While in South Africa in 1913, he swindled a Durban bank of $5,000 under the name of Ebenezer McKay and was arrested and sentenced to 18 months. Oakland authorities planned to extradite Gibson after his sentence, but California governor Hiram Johnson refused to sign the extradition papers because the travel expenses from South Africa were too steep.

In 1916, Gibson was sentenced to life imprisonment under the habitual criminal act. He was released in 1925 and promptly went to Australia where, posing as Surgeon Major Home, he was sentenced to seven years for forging a treasury warrant drawn on the South Australian government.

Gibson may have been a skilled conman and expert forger, but he was by no means a master criminal, and he spent over 40 years in prison. In July 1940, at the age of 74, while posing as Dr. Harry Cecil Darling in a London maternity hospital, he was accused of manslaughter by gross negligence in the death of a Mrs. Higginbottam. After delaying her admission to the hospital, he did nothing to help her. Gibson's entire medical treatment consisted of asking a nurse what to do. According to testimony at his trial, Gibson had spent most of the previous five years as a post- office sorter, a laborer, and a medical herbalist. He was convicted and sentenced to 10 years.

He took the name Walter Thomas Porriott after he was released, moved to Australia and married a 58-year-old widow named Bessie. Gibson died in Brisbane, Australia in 1952. Gibson was so reviled by Bessie's family that the couple's headstone reads only "Bessie, died 25th June 1957, and her husband." But his story did not end there.

In 1997, his great-great-grandson, Steve Wilson, claimed that Gibson, who was in London in 1888, was really Jack the Ripper. Gibson left London for Australia on the day the last victim of Jack the Ripper was discovered. Gibson had some medical knowledge and was known to hate prostitutes, Wilson noted.

The claim sounds dubious, but with Gibson, anything was possible.

The Father of Electrical Medicine

There is often a fine line between a quack and a visionary. Nicola Tesla, Joseph Lister, and others who were ridiculed at first, crossed that line when their discoveries were proven to be true. Dr. Albert Abrams also crossed that line -- but in the opposite direction. He was a most unlikely candidate for such a voyage.

Abrams was born in San Francisco in 1863, and his brilliance was recognized at an early age. When only 19, Abrams received a medical degree from the University of Heidelberg, then the finest medical school in the world. Abrams continued his studies in the capitals of Europe and returned to California to begin his practice. In 1889, he was elected vice-president of the California State Medical Association. In 1893, he became a full professor of pathology and director of the medical clinic of Cooper Medical College, which later became Stanford University.

From 1904 until his death, Abrams was president of the Emanu-El clinic. He helped pioneer new medical devices, such as X-rays and fluoroscopes. Abrams became a recognized expert in the field of neurology, and his books on diseases of the heart and clinical diagnoses became standards in the field. As time went on, Abrams became critical of the German-dominated medical establishment, but it wasn't until his discovery of spondylotherapy in1908 that he crossed the line from the heights of the visionary to the valley of the quacks.

Paul Drexler

The early 20th Century was a time of great developments and competing theories in medicine. Electricity was still a new discovery and was thought by many to have significant curative powers. Alternative approaches, such as chiropractic treatment and osteopathy posited that a host of diseases could be cured by bone and muscle manipulation. Abram's invention, spondylotherapy, combined both elements.

Abrams claimed that careful and repetitive stimulation of the spinal column using an electric vertical percussion vibrator could diagnose almost all medical problems. But Abrams was just getting started. He invented the dynamizer, an amazing machine that, based on a single drop of blood from a patient, could determine the illnesses afflicting the patient and the patient's age, sex, race, and even religion.

Abrams would place the blood sample of the patient in the dynamizer, which was connected to the forehead of a healthy male lab assistant, who stood stripped to the waist, facing west, under dim lighting conditions. The lab assistant was a stand-in for the actual patient, who could be hundreds of miles away. The dynamizer was switched on, and Abrams tapped the abdomen of his lab assistant, interpreting the vibratory patterns this produced into his diagnosis and personality profile.

But science marches on. Abrams then came up with a new machine, the oscilloclast, which could cure whatever illnesses the dynamizer identified. Abrams theorized that every disease has its rate of vibration and that drugs that treat these diseases also have the same vibration rate. The oscilloclast was able to produce vibrations at different rates. So, by adjusting the oscilloclast to the frequency of the curative drug, the machine would produce the therapeutic action of the drug and cure the patient. He modestly called this practice ERA or Electrical Reactions of Abrams.

Rather than sell the oscilloclasts, which were nicknamed "magic boxes," Abrams leased them to future practitioners. These practitioners, who paid $200 for training, agreed to kick back a percentage of their profits and to never open the boxes. As the money rolled in, Abrams bought a mansion in San Francisco's tony Sea Cliff district and furnished it with a library of rare books, a pipe organ, and an impressive collection of Asian art.

Though the medical establishment was outraged, Abrams did have some prominent supporters, including Sir James Barr, the former President of the British Medical Association; Upton Sinclair, a prominent writer and reformer; and Sir Arthur Conan Doyle, creator of Sherlock Holmes.

The press loved Dr. Abrams. He looked and sounded impressive, made amazing claims, and his stories sold newspapers. The papers took a "balanced" approach. Rather than investigating the truth of his claims, they would give the medical association a paragraph to attack Abrams. They would then give Abrams three paragraphs to portray himself as a pioneer besieged by jealous competitors. That kind of shoddy journalism could never happen today, of course!

In 1921, fifty years before DNA testing, a Superior Court judge used the results of Abrams's oscilloclast test to determine a child's legitimacy. The judge's action inspired a strong opposite reaction from the scientific world. UC Berkeley biochemistry professor Dr. W. Bloor replied that a blood test could only prove whether the blood is human or animal. San Francisco physician Thomas Buckley sent Abrams a sample of his own blood and that of his son and asked Abrams to determine the child's paternity. Abrams tested the blood and claimed that the sample was not human. Buckley replied, "What am I, a fish?" and took the story to the newspapers.

Scientific American spent a year investigating Abrams's claims. They sent an ERA practitioner six vials, each containing a germ culture of a specific disease and asked him to analyze the vials. The practitioner did not get a single one right. For example, he identified the vial containing pneumococcus as a combination of syphilis, tuberculosis, streptococcus, malaria and the flu.

When Nobel Prize-winning physicist R.A. Millikan examined the oscilloclast, he said, "It might have been thrown together by a ten-year-old boy who knows a little about electricity to mystify an eight-year-old old boy who knows nothing about it." The man who built the boxes told investigators that Abrams paid him thirty dollars per box and told him that the arrangement of wires inside was not important.

Under pressure and in failing health, Abrams made another prognostication. He predicted that he would die in 1924, and on January 14th of that year, he was proven correct. With Abrams's death and his theories disproven by mainstream science, you might think that

Electrical Reactions of Abrams (ERA) would disappear. But you would be forgetting two important natural laws. The first law of thermodynamics states, "Energy cannot be destroyed; it can only be transformed from one form to another." And the first law of Barnum says, "There's a sucker born every minute."

Abrams's theories and versions of his devices have been used by scores of practitioners over the last ninety years. In the 1930s, Dr. Ruth Down, a chiropractor, took Abrams's theories one step further. She created the RadioVision Instrument, a machine the size of a console radio, containing a myriad of impressive looking dials and wires. Using these dials and an electrode, she would "tune in" to the patient's organs, measuring their vibratory rate. Though she was exposed time and again, Down managed to misdiagnose over 35,000 patients in a career that lasted almost 40 years. She was under indictment for grand theft when she died in 1963.

Today Radionics is firmly entrenched in the alternative healing world along with bio photon rebalancing and the BEST life force regenerator. Amazon sells a variety of radionic-related products, including a book titled "Wishing Machines: Getting the Things You Want Through Radionic Devices."

Paul Drexler

MASTERS OF ESCAPE

Masters of escape are the rock stars of criminals; the smartest, most creative and daring convicts. Escaping from a prison where millions of dollars have been spent to keep you captive requires tremendous physical, intellectual, and psychological resources. You may have to design and build a 100-yard tunnel out of spare wood and run wires and lights from a stolen power source. You may have to swim through a cesspool, across a raging river, or make a gun out of scrap metal. It's no surprise that the majority of escape artists are also bank robbers since the traits needed for both activities are similar. Some people wonder why such gifted people don't use their ability to make a good living within the law. Willie "the Actor" Sutton, legendary 20th-century bank robber and escape artist, explains.

"I loved it. I was more alive when I was inside a bank, robbing it, than at any other time in my life. I enjoyed everything about it so much that one or two weeks later, I'd be out looking for the next job. But to me, the money was the chips, that's all."

On the run, alone, outnumbered, masters of escape arouse our sympathy and admiration despite their violent crimes. I will explore four cases where desperate California criminals thrilled the populace with their daring but ultimately paid the price.

Paul Drexler

The Literate Larcenist

A recent Department of Education survey revealed that over half of American adults over the age of 16 are functionally illiterate. Nothing more clearly illustrates this problem than the poor quality of today's holdup notes. For example:

Bank robber nabbed after handing the teller a note that read, "Give money, I gun." — via Minnesota Local News:

"This is a stickkup. Put all you muny in this bag." — Holdup note given to Bank of America teller.

By comparison, take a look at this note, which was handed to the cashier of the San Francisco Savings Bank on March 24, 1894:

"Mr. Cashier, Sir: After considering my deplorable circumstances I have decided that this life is not worth living without liberal means and therefore I am resolved to make one more effort in the high road of self-help to sustain my miserable existence. Should you not comply with my demand, I am compelled to employ my last remedy, a bottle of nitro-glycerine, and to bury myself under the ruins of this building, blasted to everlasting nothingness."

> *Yours respectfully,*
> *A despondent man*

Now, this is a holdup note to be proud of: well written, respectful, even philosophical. Unfortunately, cashier William Herrick did not see it that way. He reached into his desk and pulled out a gun. The despondent bank robber fired; his first shot went by Herrick's ear. His second shot hit Herrick's heart, killing him. Before he died, Herrick managed to get a shot off that shattered the glass in the teller's window and drove a piece into the robber's eye.

Charles Melvin, the bank's bookkeeper, pulled out a gun and opened fire on the bank robber. The bank robber dashed onto Market Street towards the Mission. Bystanders pursued him. He ran up Valencia Street, stole a horse and buggy and drove it into a blind alley on Mission and 13th streets.

He abandoned the buggy and ran into a basement at 14th Street, where a crowd surrounded the house and the police arrested him. When captured, the man was armed with two Smith and Wesson .44 caliber pistols, a cartridge belt with 50 rounds, a dirk knife, and carried a notebook written in code.

He gave his name as William Bonnement. Police suspected otherwise and searched further to identify him. On his body was an extensive tattoo panorama including ballet girls, cowboys, sailors, Indians, the Goddess of Liberty, and the American Flag. He was quickly identified as William Frederick, a notorious outlaw who had served four years at Folsom Prison. Frederick was most noted for his association with Chris Evans, John and George Sontag, famous train robbers of California's best-known railroad, the Southern Pacific.

*William Frederick mugshot
and San Quentin photograph.
(Historical Detective, 1895)*

The Southern Pacific, or SP controlled the state government for 30 years through wholesale bribery and corruption. It had received millions of acres and dollars from the government to build the tracks and was a powerful monopoly, charging whatever it wanted for carrying freight. In Northern California, the railroad encouraged settlers on its land in Tulare County and said it would sell the land to the settlers in a few years for $2.50 an acre. But when the SP railroad decided to sell the land in 1878, it jacked up the price to $25 an acre and threatened to evict those who would not pay.

The farmers formed the Settlers League to fight the railroads. On May 11, 1880, in Hanford, California, members of the Settlers League confronted railroad men who were evicting settlers, and a gunfight broke out. When the shooting stopped, five settlers and two of the railroad men were dead. The gunfight became known as the "Mussel Shoals Massacre" and caused most farmers to despise the Southern Pacific railroad.

When farmers Chris Evans, John Sontag, and his brother George began holding up S.P. trains, they were seen as folk heroes by the locals. When the gang held up a train in Fresno, witnesses identified their team of horses as belonging to Evans and Sontag. George was arrested a few days later, but Evans and Sontag escaped. In 1892, a huge manhunt began for the men, who were hidden by local supporters.

Eve Evans, Chris's daughter, overheard talk that a posse knew where her father was hiding. She followed the posse and fired a shot, which alerted her father and enabled him to escape. Twice Evans and Sontag shot it out with their pursuers, killing a sheriff and two posse members in the exchange of gunfire. But their time was running out. On June 26,1893 a posse ambushed the train robbers, mortally wounding John Sontag and wounding Evans, who was captured a few weeks later.

In early June, William Frederick smuggled three guns into Folsom prison to help George Sontag escape. The guns were hidden in the rock quarry, where many of the prisoners worked. On June 28, learning that his brother had been captured and was seriously wounded, George and five other convicts decided to escape. They grabbed guard Lieutenant Frank Briarre, took his gun and forced him to accompany them to the rocks where their guns were hidden. The other guards were afraid to fire on the convicts while they were holding Briarre. Suddenly, Briarre jumped aside and the guards started firing. The prisoners responded, but they were outflanked and outgunned.

Warden Aull had heard rumors of an escape attempt and had hired extra marksmen to work at the prison. He had also arranged for Gatling guns, an early version of a machine gun, to be concealed in the quarry area. Sharpshooters raked the prisoners with Gatling guns and rifles. After fifty minutes, the prisoners surrendered. Three prisoners were dead and three were seriously wounded, including George Sontag.

William Frederick was no folk hero. He confessed to a friend that he had murdered at least five people including a sheriff, a train brakeman, and three Chinese miners. Frederick's decoded notebook revealed evidence of additional crimes, formulas for bomb making, and an interest in phrenology, the pseudoscience of the study of the skull and its relationship to personality and behavior. Police considered him a serious escape risk.

Despite his background, or perhaps because of it, Frederick was visited by legions of female admirers in jail. In April 1894, his attorney and a heavily veiled young woman visited him in his cell. She gave her name as Miss Evans. After they left, the head jailor realized that Miss Evans was Eva Evans, the daughter of the notorious train robber Chris Evans. She had visited her father before his successful escape. The jailor searched the cell carefully and found two holes cut into the cell next door. Frederick's plan was to break into the cell next door and escape. He was moved into a solid steel cell.

Yet Frederick somehow got out of his cell on April 5, attacked a jailor, and reached an outer door before other guards overcame him.

At his trial, his attorney tried the following arguments:

- Frederick shot Herrick in self-defence since Herrick pulled a gun on him.

- Herrick was killed accidentally by the bank's bookkeeper, Charles Melvin.

- Frederick was insane, and therefore not guilty.

The jury rejected these arguments, and Frederick was convicted of murder and sentenced to death. During his sentencing, Frederick screamed and howled constantly, trying to convince authorities of his unsound mind. Three psychiatrists testified that Frederick was sane.

Public interest in Frederick continued even after his conviction. A team of phrenologists measured his skull and declared that his measurements showed that he was "ruthless, combative, but had a fine sense of parental love and a highly developed love of art and poetry."

The phrenologists' predictions were proven accurate just a few months later.

"Murderer Frederick Chloroformed for Reciting Original Poetry," read a subhead of a December 9, 1894, article in the San Francisco Chronicle. The article related that the combative Frederick had been put in a straitjacket after setting his mattress on fire and that his epic poem about the Folsom Prison jailbreak had ended with his sedation.

By July 25, 1895, Frederick had regained his equilibrium. On his last night alive, Frederick tried to sell his confession to a reporter for $100 so he could buy a decent headstone, but he was insulted when the offer was only $20.

Frederick's hanging went off without a hitch. The widow of Herrick, Frederick's victim, received $5,000 from the San Francisco Savings Bank as compensation.

King of the Escape Artists

Fame is fleeting whether you're a rock star, a movie star, or a criminal. One day you're in the front-page headlines, the next day you're yesterday's news. This was the sad story of Roy Gardner. Roy Gardner, known as "King of the Escape Artists," was the most admired criminal in America for two years. His good looks, his daring, and his open disposition charmed even his victims.

Born in 1886, Roy craved adventure from a young age. In 1905, after two years in the army, Roy became a soldier of fortune and tried to smuggle guns to the rebels during the Mexican revolution. Unfortunately, he was captured by government forces and was sentenced to death. He escaped, using a knife to saw through a wooden door in his cell, and made his way back to the United States. For the next few years, he traveled around the west, boxing under the name of "Young Fitzsimmons" and doing other odd jobs

In 1911, out of funds in San Francisco, Roy committed his first crime. He snatched a tray of diamond rings from a jeweler on Market Street and ran. He was captured a few minutes later in front of John's Grill and was sentenced to five years in San Quentin. He saved the life of a prison guard during a riot and was rewarded with an early parole in 1913. Given a second chance, Roy became a skilled welder, got married and had a child. Like Joseph in Egypt, seven years of abundance followed. By 1920, he had saved over

$2,000, enough to buy a house. To celebrate, he decided to take his family to Tijuana for a vacation.

Within two days, he had lost all his money at the racetrack and was desperate. While at the post office in San Diego, Roy learned that $30,000 in cash would be sent by mail to Los Angeles. He commandeered the mail truck after it left the station, stole the mailbags and returned to a room he had rented on Front Street. He found $131,000 in cash and Canadian bonds inside the bags. Roy stuffed the money into his clothes, went out on the town and checked into a room at San Diego's Redding Hotel.

At breakfast the next day, Gardner was shocked to see his name in the headlines as the mail bandit. Police had discovered the empty mailbags and a suitcase with his name on it in his Front Street room. Gardner fled to Del Mar where he was captured the next day and all the money was recovered. Roy was convicted of armed mail robbery and sentenced to 25 years at Washington's McNeil Island prison. On June 5, 1920, as the train drove through the rugged country in Oregon, Roy distracted the guard, disarmed him, and leaped from the train. Using a stolen motorboat, motorcycle, and car as his escape vehicles Gardner traveled to Iowa where he got a job as a welding inspector. But he missed his family, and in April 1921, he returned to California, slipped past the police watching the house, and had a brief reunion with his wife and daughter.

Returning to crime, Gardner robbed a Southern Pacific mail train of $100,000 and made his way to Roseville, California. Ever the gambler, Roy joined a poker game in the back room of the Porter House hotel.

He was so intent on the game that he didn't notice the detectives surrounding him until he was arrested. Gardner pled guilty in San Francisco, and the court added 25 more years to his sentence.

He was put on the train to prison, this time guarded by two deputies and chained to another convict. During the trip, Roy retrieved a gun an associate had hidden in the bathroom, got the drop on his guards and escaped. As rain poured down, Roy hid in the underbrush in Castle Rock, Washington. After three days, starving and weak, Gardner hopped a train to Centralia, Oregon, where he was recaptured and taken to McNeil Island.

Roy's escapes had made him famous, and his devoted wife, Dolly, and three-year-old daughter, Jean, made good copy for the newspapers. In June 1921, Dolly wrote a column for the San Francisco Call. "I have set beside my own sense of judgment and criticism for I know in my heart that Roy is just a great reckless boy. He has always been crazy about adventure...I am quite sure I will wait for him even for fifty years because he is the love of my life..."

On September 5, while everyone was watching a prison baseball game at McNeil Island, Roy and two other men made a break for the fence. Guards fired, killing one of the other men and severely wounding the other. Roy was shot twice in the legs but made it over the fence and hid in the thick brush while guards searched around him.

Roy slipped back during the night and hid in the prison barn, drinking milk from the cows while authorities frantically searched outside the walls. Luckily for Roy, he received only flesh wounds from the bullets, and in the next two days, he recovered enough to continue his escape. On September 8, Gardner swam three miles to neighboring Fox Island and escaped the area.

On September 26, the San Francisco Bulletin published a letter Roy sent to them in which he expressed his regret and vowed to reform. He even wrote to President Harding asking for clemency. "Please, Mr. Harding. Just one more chance," he begged.

On November 15, an unreformed Roy tried to rob the mail train as it left Phoenix, Arizona, but this time the result was different. Herbert Inderlied, the postal clerk, fought back and overpowered Gardner.

Gardner was convicted and sent to Leavenworth Prison, where he spent 13 years. In 1934, with the kind of bad judgment that marked his career, Gardner volunteered to go to Alcatraz to serve the rest of his sentence closer to his family. Alcatraz was by far the toughest prison in the United States, and when Gardner was released in 1936, he was a broken man. His wife, Dolly, after 15 years of waiting, had divorced him and remarried.

Roy wrote an autobiography --"Hellcatraz" -- which detailed his life and his time in Alcatraz, but the public had forgotten him. In 1940, broke and in bad health, he dropped a pellet of cyanide in a cup in the bathroom of his Turk Street room, inhaled the fumes and died.

Manhunt: The Joe Tanko Story

Wanted poster for Joe Tanko and Floyd Hall.
(California State archives, 1926)

There is nothing more exciting than a good manhunt. A notorious criminal is on the run. His picture stares out from the front page of the newspapers with a large reward attached. A frisson of excitement runs through the city. At any moment, this desperado could appear, die in a shootout with police or escape again into the shadows. When it came to being hunted, there was no man better than Joe Tanko.

It all began in September 1923 when 24- year-old Tanko and his 21-year-old crime partner, Floyd Hall, fatally shot San Bruno Police Chief Arthur G. Meehan. They were caught a few weeks later when Tanko's brother Dan gave police a letter from Joe in which Tanko admitted to 40 robberies and to killing Meehan.

Because of their youth and their guilty plea, Tanko and Hall were spared the death penalty and received a life sentence instead. Tanko always blamed his brother for his arrest and threatened to kill him.

While being transported to San Quentin, the crime partners made their first escape attempt but were foiled by an alert sheriff. A year later, on April 7, 1925, Tanko and Hall broke out of San Quentin by picking a lock and sliding down a jute rope. While police and armed posses searched for them, Tanko and Hall provisioned themselves with food, supplies, and firearms from store burglaries in Petaluma and Healdsburg. The pair then embarked on a spectacular crime spree.

On April 12, they carjacked a Santa Rosa rancher; on April 14, they held up a Sacramento cab driver and escaped after a shootout with Sacramento Police. A few days later, while police staked out the highways around California's capital city, Tanko and Hall robbed Harry Litzberg's Sacramento store, killing him in the process.

Police from neighboring communities flooded into Sacramento to aid the search, but to no avail. On April 21, Tanko and Hall continued their depredations, robbing two cab drivers and commandeering their cars. Two days later, at 17th and Q Street, they entered the car where Frank Harlow and his four-year-old daughter were sitting and forced Harlow to drive them out of town. As police chased them, Tanko fired into the pursuing car, severely wounding police officer Clyde Nunn. The fugitives drove on until the car ran out of gas, and then they fled on foot, leaving Harlow and his daughter unharmed. They were reported to be in Auburn, then in Grass Valley. A massive manhunt pursued them; posses searched the surrounding swamps, and riverbanks without success.

On May 5, the pair commandeered a U.S. Mail truck in the town of Gold Run and made a wild drive down the mountain towards Sacramento. They abandoned the truck when a tire went flat and they disappeared into the foothills. Over 1,000 armed pursuers surrounded the area in what was called the "Siege of the Sierras."

It was the greatest manhunt in California history. "It seems impossible for them to have broken through the surrounding posses and we expect to fight it out with them soon after daylight," declared Placer County's sheriff. But Tanko and Hall doubled back during the night and slipped through the dragnet. They stole a car and re- entered Sacramento on May 14. Federal and state authorities placed a reward of $6,100 on their heads.

At this point, Hall and Tanko decided that their chances were better if they separated. Hall was arrested the next day when an ex-con, in whose room he was hiding, turned him over to police for the reward money. Tanko disappeared.

While hundreds of armed men searched every rooming house in Sacramento, Tanko was reported heading for the Bay Area. As accountant C.O Buntly drove slowly through Golden Gate Park on May 19, a man entered his car and stuck a gun into his side. It was Joe Tanko. "Drive like hell! I don't care where to," he commanded. Buntly drove to North Beach, and when the car became stuck in traffic on Kearny Street, Tanko jumped out and escaped.

By this time, both men had achieved near mythic status. Hall was treated like a celebrity by a fawning press. "Captured desperado sobs at mention of his family," was the subhead of an article in the San Francisco Examiner. While Tanko was still at large, Hall was indicted for the murder of Litzberg and the shooting of Officer Nunn. Hall was the ultimate "bad boy," fearless, charming, and photogenic. He was convicted and sentenced to death, but the guilty verdict was reversed on appeal and a second trial was scheduled.

Where was Tanko? For most of the next 18 months, Tanko lived in Denver, supporting himself through robberies and other criminal activities. He kept his identity a secret and told his girlfriend he was a San Francisco businessman. He returned to San Francisco in October 1926 to see his other girlfriend, a woman who knew his secret.

On November 13, SFPD Sergeant Vernon Van Matre stood outside a basement apartment at 1373 McAllister Street preparing to arrest Willie De Bardalaben and his gang for an assault on a man and his wife. Van Matre did not expect trouble, but he brought along three other policemen to block the other exits in case Willie decided to make a run for it. Van Matre raised an outside window and saw De Bardelaben stretched out on a bed. He called out to Willie, telling him that the building was surrounded and that he should come out with his hands up.

The suspect rose with his hands up and backed away from the officer saying, "I can't. He's got me covered." As Van Matre shoved aside the screen to enter the room he was shot in the groin by Joe Tanko, who had been hiding out in the apartment. Tanko took the stairway leading to rooms above.

As he climbed the stairs, Tanko came face to face with Detective Sergeant Earl Roney, who told him to surrender. Tanko fired first, hitting Roney in the stomach. Though wounded seriously, Roney fired back five times, killing Tanko instantly.

When news of the shooting got out, crowds filled McAllister Street, reveling vicariously in the recent drama. Almost 20,000 people visited the Coroner's office over the next few days, eager to view the corpse of the man who had terrified Northern California. "He's smaller than I thought he'd be," was the most popular observation. Tanko was buried in Potter's Field in San Mateo.

With Tanko dead and Hall in prison for life and facing another murder trial, it would seem that the story was over. But the story reckoned without Floyd Hall. In his second trial, despite eyewitness testimony, Hall was acquitted of the shooting of Officer Nunn. His courtroom groupies cheered mightily. After a second trial on the Litzberg murder proved inconclusive, authorities decided not to retry him, since he was already serving a life sentence for the murder of Police Chief Mehan. But sometimes you can't keep a bad man down.

In 1928, Hall made a rope out of blankets and darkened his face to appear black in an unsuccessful escape attempt. Ten years later, Hall's wife smuggled a gun into the prison in yet another attempted jailbreak. With a record like this, it was no surprise that his parole was turned down numerous times. But Hall was persistent, and in 1956, at the age of 51, he was paroled. But Hall still had his charm.

In 1972, Floyd Hall, who had committed over 40 armed robberies, murdered a police chief and a storekeeper, received a full pardon from Governor Ronald Reagan with the help of a lobbyist who fell under Hall's charm. Retired Sacramento attorney Ed Farrell recalled, "They took him to the Brass Rail, a lobbyist and legislative hangout, and Hall got acquainted with everyone within an hour. He was very personable."

> *"I am bewitched with the rogue's company. If the rascal has not given me medicines to make me love him, I'll be hanged."*
>
> —William Shakespeare

The Yacht Bandits

Ethan McNabb, Folsom Prison, 1925
(California State archives, 1933)

Lloyd Sampsell, Folsom Prison, 1933
(California State archives, 1933)

Lloyd Sampsell and Ethan McNabb were both cut from the same well-tailored cloth. They were brilliant, multi-talented and ruthless. They could do almost anything: sail a yacht, write a sonnet or make a working gun out of metal scraps. They could do anything, except go straight. Known as the "Yacht Bandits," Sampsell and McNabb were two of the most accomplished men ever executed by the State of California.

Lloyd Sampsell was born on April 4, 1900, in Seattle to a family of wanderers, always looking for the American dream. Life was boom or bust for the family until they reached California in 1907. His father was a hard-driving restaurateur, who achieved success in Los Angeles. Lloyd was headstrong and impulsive and clashed with his exacting father. Sampsell dropped out of school at 15 and joined the Navy, but he received a dishonorable discharge after one year. Lloyd was convicted of forgery in Missouri in 1917, but he escaped from the youth authority and joined his father in Los Angeles two years later.

Ethan McNabb and the wild town of Deadwood, South Dakota, were made for each other, but he was born thirty years too late. Arrested in Deadwood at the age of eleven in 1908, Ethan was already living like an outlaw. He led a gang of boys, slept in a cave outside of town, and supported himself by stealing. According to the Deadwood Argus-Leader: "His father declares that he can do nothing with him and has lost control of him. The boy smokes cigarettes and sometimes remains away from his home all night." McNabb was sent to a reform school (then known as an industrial school) for three years. He moved to Los Angeles when he was about 20 years old. McNabb's mechanical aptitude helped get him a job as a bosun for American President Lines, and he became an accomplished sailor. He was also a chauffeur for Grace Darmond, a popular movie star of the silent film era. But the pull of life outside the law was too strong, and he turned to robbery.

McNabb and his partner J.W. Cave committed over100 armed highway robberies before their dramatic capture in July 1922. The men were driving a stolen armored car in San Francisco when two cops who had been tailing them jumped on the car's running board, surprising the bandits. The car contained two revolvers, an automatic pistol, and a shotgun with 300 rounds of ammunition. Newspapers described both men as "stylishly dressed and had more the appearance of prosperous young businessmen than desperate bandits." McNabb was convicted of two counts of armed robbery and sent to Folsom Prison.

Sampsell was arrested for bigamy and bank robbery in 1923. By then he already exhibited the charm and personality that was to win over so many people. A letter of recommendation to Lloyd's father from the president of the bank Sampsell robbed illustrates this. "I will be glad to give you any assistance in this matter for I do not feel that the boy is a real criminal. I believe he will make good if given the opportunity."

Sampsell and McNabb met in Folsom prison, recognized their shared abilities, and decided to become partners. Cheerfully unrepentant upon their release from jail in 1927, they continued their crooked ways, using their intelligence and daring to rise to the top of the criminal fraternity. In 1928, Sampsell and

McNabb led a conspiracy to smuggle guns and 1,000,000 rounds of ammunition to rebels in Mexico.

When the scheme fell through, the partners in crime purchased a fifty-foot yacht, which they named The Sovereign, and used it to smuggle alcohol into California. Sampsell's beautiful wife, Lita, joined them as they sailed in style from Vancouver to Los Angeles, posing as wealthy yachtsmen. They even became members of the exclusive St. Francis Yacht Club in San Francisco. The Sovereign served as the world's most lavish getaway vehicle for their real business: bank robbery. By some estimates, it appears that the pair robbed as many as 100 banks netting well over $200,000 (almost $3 million dollars in today's money).

In early June 1929, San Francisco police got a tip that the yacht bandits had shipped an expensive automobile from Seattle to an address in San Francisco. Detectives staked out the apartment and arrested the trio when they arrived. A stash of high-powered rifles, automatic weapons and $10,000 in gold stolen from a Berkeley bank were in the apartment.

Yacht Seizure Breaks Up Bandit Gang

San Francisco Chronicle 1925

Yacht Bandits Captured! Three Alleged Super Crooks Believed to Have Plied Pacific Coast Cities from San Diego to Vancouver in Luxuriously Appointed Yacht" screamed the headlines. Police freed Lita a few weeks later when they decided she had nothing to do with the crimes.

The Yacht Bandits had committed crimes in so many jurisdictions that the question of where they should be tried became an issue. It was decided to try them where there was the most evidence and the best prosecutor. The place was Alameda County, and the prosecutor was Earl Warren, the future chief justice of the United States.

While waiting for the trial, Sampsell tried unsuccessfully to escape the Alameda jail. The trial didn't go well either; it was an open and shut case. Six witnesses from the bank identified Sampsell and McNabb as the stickup men. The strongbox from the Bank of America was recovered from their Leavenworth Street apartment. Inside the strongbox were travelers' checks with serial numbers matching those stolen from the bank. The men were convicted and sent to Folsom Prison for 15 years.

Sampsell and McNabb had no intention of staying incarcerated for even 15 months, and they immediately started plotting their escape. The idea was simple. Sampsell and McNabb would hide in the prison. After days of fruitless searching, the authorities would assume they had escaped and concentrate the manhunt outside the prison. With security in the prison back to normal, Sampsell and McNabb would be smuggled out.

Finding a hiding place that could withstand days of round-the-clock searching would be an extreme challenge. Folsom was one of the top maximum-security prisons in the United States and was built to be escape proof. Sampsell conceived a plan that was technically brilliant and incredibly dangerous.

He had inmate Ben Richardson build a special box. The box was 4 ½ feet wide, 7 ½ feet long and 4 feet high, equipped with electric lights with storage batteries, reading matter, food, and water. It was located under Richardson's locker in the blacksmith shop where he worked. On June 6, 1930, Sampsell and McNabb clambered into the box. Richardson covered the box with 18 inches of dirt and then replaced the floor of his locker. Sampsell and McNabb were now buried alive with enough provisions and air to last a week. They had paid two prison officials $12,000 to smuggle them out when the coast was clear. When Sampsell and McNabb went missing that evening, Warden Smith locked down the prison. He kept all the prisoners in their cells while he ordered a thorough search of the prison.

A statewide search was ordered, and police kept a close eye on Lita Sampsell's house in case the escapees went there. After seven days, however, Sampsell and McNabb were betrayed by the bribed prison officials who claimed they were tipped off by an unnamed inmate. When Sampsell and McNabb were discovered, they were so weak from lack of air and food, they were unable to stand. The pair spent the next six months in solitary confinement.

They tried again in 1932. Detroit gangster James Palese and Emil Colson smuggled guns and rifles into Folsom. Emil's brother, Martin, also in Folsom, was to be part of the escape. Three of the guns were discovered in a wooden barrow and the plot failed. At this point, authorities split up the two men, sending McNabb to San Quentin.

At Folsom in 1933, Lloyd Sampsell secretly built two working pistols in the prison workshop out of an air compressor pipe and other spare parts. Sampsell and Martin Colson used the guns to capture five employees in the administration building and forced the men to ask the warden to meet them. The Warden was suspicious and ordered armed guards to surround the building. When the escapers and the warden stepped into the yard, they were surrounded and Sampsell was disarmed. Seeing what was happening, Colson shot himself in the head with his homemade gun and died. Sampsell was badly beaten and again put into solitary confinement for a year.

Ethan McNabb, doing his time in San Quentin, was not far behind. In 1934, he manufactured his own guns and ammunition and led three other prisoners in an escape attempt. On a foggy evening, they captured a guard and McNabb put on his uniform. McNabb took a shot at a tower guard who challenged him – but missed, and the escape failed. But the plotters accidentally killed a convict. Because McNabb was facing a life sentence, the Yacht Bandit was charged with a capital crime. He was convicted and sentenced to death.

As his execution date approached, McNabb asked that he receive a naval burial and have his body wrapped in canvas and dropped into the ocean. He explained, with heavy sarcasm, "This should be pleasing to the good citizens of California who have striven so assiduously to terminate my sojourn among them. They shall be pleased to know that no honest native shall be forced to burrow into the ground of the fair state to scoop out a trench for my weary bones." In the last two weeks of his life, McNabb wrote a book, which he gave to his attorney. On the night before his execution, McNabb calmly read a book on steam fitting. On September 6, 1935, Ethan McNabb nonchalantly approached the gallows, quoted a passage from Hillaire Belloc's "Mercy of Allah" and was executed.

At Folsom, Sampsell faced a different future. Convicts armed with homemade knives surrounded Warden Clarence Larkin and Captain of the Guards, William Ryan, on September 19, 1937. An inmate held a knife to Larkin's neck and yelled, "Open the gates and let us out. Any interference and we'll kill the warden."

"Don't open the gates," shouted Larkin, "even if they kill me." Realizing that their plan had failed, the cons stabbed Larkin and Ryan. The guards opened fire killing two of the escapers and two other prisoners. The rest were captured and later executed. Larkin died of his wounds a few days later, but Ryan recovered.

Ryan, who had shed a quart of his own blood in defense of the prison, expected to be named Larkin's replacement. But at that time, wardens were politically appointed, and the governor wanted the job to go to someone from Southern California. Clyde Plummer, who had been an investigator for the District Attorney in Los Angeles, was selected as warden. Ryan was bitterly resentful.

The two men also had markedly different ideas about prison. Ryan strongly believed that prison was a place where men should be warehoused and punished. Most of the guards felt the same way and supported Ryan.

Plummer, on the other hand, was open to the possibility of reform so that the men could eventually return to society. Plummer's attempts to make prison less punitive were scoffed at by traditionalists. When Plummer agreed to have the convict orchestra play at dinnertime the Stockton Independent said, "Warden Clyde Plummer of Folsom is apparently under the impression that he is a Gilbert and Sullivan prison warden, and is handling men who will dance off the stage at the end of their act and become ordinary citizens. "

Prisons are complex organisms, controlled by hundreds of formal and informal rules and sources of power. A warden needs a certain level of consent from powerful prisoners, who act as the informal leaders. In the California of the 1930s, this meant the con boss system. In the con boss system, the more powerful convicts are given additional power and responsibilities to help manage the kitchen, laundry, and other units.

A prison guard put it this way. "Every department has to have somebody that you have to hold responsible, because they will keep the others working, and they will keep the stealing down to a minimum."

Lloyd Sampsell was a natural pick for con boss. He was an influential presence at Folsom and a talented writer, a skill he used to teach many of the other convicts to read. Many of the guards were illiterate as well, and Sampsell tutored them to help them pass civil service tests. He became con boss in charge of the education department.

Since Warden Plummer had a strained relationship with the guards, he developed a stronger connection with the con bosses, including Sampsell. Because of this relationship, no guards ever confronted or challenged Sampsell. He came and went as he pleased and managed to stay on good terms with Captain Ryan and the guards.

The war years were eventful for Sampsell. He found a French connection, gained temporary freedom and accidentally changed California's correctional system.

His wife, Lita, never visited him in prison, but his writing brought a new woman into his life. Jacqueline

De La Prevotiere, a French exile working as a translator for the BBC, read a book of poetry that Sampsell had written and began to correspond with him. She began visiting him at Folsom and became yet another person seduced by his little-boy-lost charm. "He interested me psychologically," she said. "I don't think Lloyd is a criminal at heart. He had a bad upbringing. He has a very confused idea that he had to get even with the world for the injustice it has done him."

So many men had been drafted during World War II that farms needed workers to pick the crops. Harvest camps were set up to ease the shortage, and inmates became farmworkers. Working in a harvest camp was a treasured assignment. The food was much better than prison chow and the rules were less strict. Only non-violent convicts with good prison records were supposed to go to harvest camps. On paper, Sampsell was ineligible. But it was easy in the con boss world. Sampsell got himself transferred to a harvest camp near Davis.

Security at the camp was lax. Inmates snuck into local bars and drank. Gambling was common. But Sampsell carried this freedom to a new level. He lived in a private bunkhouse away from the other prisoners and traveled freely on the weekends. His trips included an American Legion dance, shopping trips to Davis and Sacramento, and even the Top of the Mark in San Francisco, excursions financed by his poker winnings.

But Lloyd's main San Francisco destination was an apartment on Bush Street where De La Prevotiere lived. He would leave camp at two in the afternoon and return at five the next morning. He often left her apartment phone number in camp in case he needed to be reached. Jacqueline visited him at the camp numerous times. After six months, someone turned Sampsell in, and San Francisco police arrested him at Jacqueline's apartment.

Governor Earl Warren, who had put Sampsell in jail in 1929, called it "the most outrageous thing I have ever heard of in prison management," and said that the prison was being run by the inmates. The prison scandal was front- page news, the camps were closed, and Warden Plummer was forced to resign. Warren convened a series of correction department hearings that led to major changes in the state penal administration.

Finally, in 1947, after 18 years in prison Sampsell was paroled. He remarried Lita, much to the anger of his girlfriend Jacqueline. His father had a job waiting for him managing one of his restaurants. But reform was not in Lloyd's DNA. He teamed with Ben Richardson, who had helped with the 1930 escape, and started robbing banks again. Sampsell, who had taught Richardson to read, dominated the relationship, gave the orders, and took the lion's share of the money.

Lloyd always considered himself the consummate professional bank robber and had prided himself on the fact that, in over 100 bank robberies, he had never used a gun. He had the ability to intimidate and reassure his bank robbery victims. A bank manager recalled that after showing the gun, Sampsell gave "the assurance that he did not want to hurt me or anyone else in the bank.... After that, I felt that the transaction was more of a business deal than anything else."

But in March 1948, during a robbery at the Seaboard Finance Company in San Diego, the unexpected happened. Sampsell had gotten the contents of the cash drawers and the safe and was on his way out of the bank when a customer tried to get to the door first. In the struggle, Arthur Smith, a bank employee, grabbed Sampsell's head and neck. If it had been twenty years earlier, with McNabb by his side, the outcome would likely have been much different. But Sampsell was almost 50 and unused to opposition. Sampsell pulled out his gun and fired three times, killing Smith, and escaped.

Sampsell was put on the FBI's 10 Most Wanted list. He continued robbing banks until he was recognized and captured a year later while getting off a plane in Arizona. He was convicted and sentenced to death in the gas chamber. While on death row in San Quentin, he became good friends with another celebrity criminal, Caryl Chessman, who was then writing "Cell 2455 Death Row." The book became a best seller in 1954 and brought the issue of capital punishment front and center in public consciousness. Sampsell and Chessman became the leaders of death row. Sampsell's appeals ran out on April 25, 1952.

The night before his execution, Sampsell talked to reporters. "'They say I have led a wasted life, but I have a son. ...He's six-foot-three and 170 lbs. He's married, got two kids. He's in the service, overseas right now. So I have left something good." The next day, just before the gas took its effect, he turned to the nearly one hundred witnesses gathered and winked.

Paul Drexler

UNSOLVED MYSTERIES

Mystery (including thriller and true crime books) is by far the most popular genre in publishing. A terrible crime is committed, but by who? A detective must solve the puzzle and demystify the mystery. The villain is clever, even diabolical, but we know that in the end -- through brilliant deduction, hard work, tenacity, and luck -- the crime will be solved, the villain punished, and justice will prevail.

But real life is different. In the Zodiac case, evil triumphs, real people are hurt and killed, and the mystery remains. The boastful Zodiac, whose imprisonment is richly deserved, remains unknown and may still be out there. His victims are still unavenged. This both angers and thrills us. We feel impelled to solve this case, knowing that the person who does will be seen as the 21st century Sherlock Holmes.

The Preparedness Day bombing, the worst act of terrorism in San Francisco history, was compounded by the city's most notorious frame-up. Was the real killer a union man or a member of a shadowy anarchist group?

The real identity of S.W. Erdnase, the man who wrote magic's most famous textbook, is magic's greatest mystery. On top of that literary mystery is a greater one from real life: He may have been a serial killer.

Paul Drexler

Was he Erdnase?

MILTON FRANKLIN ANDREWS

*Milton F.Andrews was a murderer.
But was he also the mysterious Erdnase?
(SF Examiner, 1902)*

It is November 6, 1905. Police have surrounded a house at 748 McAllister Street in San Francisco's Fillmore District. Hiding inside is Milton F.Andrews, a notorious card shark and probable serial killer. But was he also "Erdnase," author of the greatest book on magic ever written? The search for Erdnase is one of the greatest and most controversial mysteries in the history of magic. It is not, however, the only mystery in this case.

Milton Andrews, born in Connecticut in 1872, developed an early interest in magic and card manipulation and became a professional gambler at age 18. By 1900, he had developed into one of the best card sharks in the country.

In 1902, a man calling himself S.W. Erdnase self-published "The Expert at the Card Table." The 143-page book explained and demonstrated the "shuffles," "shifts," and sleight-of-hand techniques used by card sharks and magicians. The first edition sold poorly, and the author reduced the price to $1 per copy.

By 1903, Andrews was at the peak of his career, claiming an annual income of over $20,000 (worth $600,000 today). But life as a card hustler had taken its toll. Andrews had developed serious digestive problems and a raging temper.

He took up with Bessie Boutin, a prostitute with a taste for luxury. They fought frequently over her drinking and his jealousy. Bessie disappeared in Denver in 1904, and Andrews left town with her jewelry. When her body was discovered, he became the main suspect in her death. Andrews was later linked to two other unsolved murders.

In November, Andrews met a woman named Nulda Olivia, who was to be his lifetime companion. The couple fled to Australia where they met William Ellis, a crooked jockey who became their gambling partner. When their victims grew suspicious, the trio took their winnings and booked passage back to America. Andrews and Olivia rented a cottage in Berkeley under the name of Brush, and Ellis stayed in a nearby hotel. Milton's health had worsened, and he was living entirely on bread, health food, and malted milk.

His jealousy turned deadly when he thought that Ellis had designs on Olivia. On October 11, Andrews invited Ellis for lunch at his cottage. He crept behind Ellis during the meal and brought a large hammer down on his head. It was a blow that would have killed an ordinary man, but Ellis had an unusually thick skull, and he was able to escape. Milton and Nulda hastily gathered their valuables and fled to San Francisco.

The attack was front-page news, and when police learned Andrew's real identity, a massive manhunt was initiated. Because of Andrew's health issues, police kept a close watch on all the health food stores. Nulda rented a room at 748 McAllister Street posing as a single woman. A few weeks later, the owner of a local grocery store told police that a single woman was buying large amounts of bread and malted milk. Police put the rooming house under surveillance and saw the shadow of a tall, thin man behind the curtains in her room. Andrews, feeling that the net was closing around him, sent the San Francisco Examiner a rambling letter denying the murder charges against him and justifying his attack on Ellis.

Two policemen entered the rooming house the next night and pounded on her door. "You will enter at your peril," Nulda cried. Moments later, two shots rang out from within the apartment. When police entered, they found the bodies of Milton Andrews and Nulda Olivia. The corpses were taken to the police morgue for identification, which was where the first mystery of the case emerged.

Two women looked at what police assumed was Nulda's body, but identified the corpse as Eva Howard.

The next day, John Gallagher, manager of the Langham Hotel, also identified the body as Eva Howard, the daughter of legendary master criminal Howard "Plunger" Howard. Howard was a racehorse owner and Australian criminal wanted for swindling and attempted murder.

Howard had lived in splendor with his family in San Francisco but vanished in 1899 when authorities discovered that he was an escaped Australian criminal named Albert Hayes. His wife and daughter, Eva, continued to live in luxury at the Langham Hotel until they disappeared a year later. The identification of Nulda Olivia as Eva Howard was later disputed. Her death certificate lists her as "Unknown Woman. She and Milton Andrews were buried near each other in unmarked graves in Mount Olivet Cemetery in Colma, just south of San Francisco.

By 1905, "The Expert at the Card Table" was back in print and rapidly making its way through magic circles. Over time, the book -- often called "The Bible" -- became the most famous, the most influential book ever published on the art of conjuring. The biblical comparison is appropriate; magicians argue about "The Open Shift" with the same ferocity that Christians disputed the divinity of Christ.

There are a number of reasons for the book's importance. Most previous books on card manipulation were exposés aimed at warning the unwary about card cheats and their techniques. But the books only pointed out what the trick looked like, not how to do it. The "Expert at the Card Table" was the first book that explained clearly how to master and perform sophisticated card conjuring. In fact, the first title of the book was "Artifice, Ruse, and Subterfuge at the Card Table – A Treatise on the Science and Art of Manipulating Cards."

The second reason for its success was the efforts of Dai "The Professor" Vernon (1894-1992), one of the most influential magicians of the 20th century. Magic, like other medieval art forms, is best transmitted from master to apprentice. Vernon, whose card tricks baffled Harry Houdini, studied with legendary magician Harry Kellar and developed some of the most famous conjuring tricks of modern magic. By the age of 13, Vernon had memorized "The Expert at the Card Table." Vernon often quoted from the book during his 30- year reign as the Magician-in-Residence at the Magic Castle in Los Angeles. His students included many of today's most celebrated magicians, such as Ricky Jay, Michael Ammar, Doug Henning, and John Carney, "The Expert at the Card Table" has been published in over 40 editions, translated into five languages, and has inspired a string quartet, a musical, and a play. But the author identity remains unknown. Investigators believed S.W Erdnase is an anagram of the author's real name. Spelled backward, it is E. S. Andrews.

Martin Gardner, who wrote a puzzle column for Scientific American, interviewed the book's illustrator, Marshall Smith, in the 1940s and concluded that Erdnase was Milton F. Andrews. Many magicians were horrified by the idea that magic's "bible" was written by a murderer and sought alternative candidates.

A first edition of the book sold for over $10,000 in 2000. This spurred additional research and speculation.

Today the leading possibilities include a mining engineer named W.E. Sanders, a railroad agent named Edwin Summers Andrews, and a con artist named E.S. Andrews, whose names are also anagrams of S.W. Erdnase.

Ricky Jay, who used one of Erdnase's classic tricks and patter in his award-winning Broadway show, "Ricky Jay and his 52 Assistants," has studied the evidence extensively without reaching a conclusion.

Chances are the identity of S.W. Erdnase, like Jack the Ripper and The Zodiac Killer, will never be known.

Paul Drexler

The Preparedness Day Bombing

One hundred years ago, everyone knew who Tom Mooney was. Just mentioning his name could start an argument. To many, he was a political prisoner -- a labor martyr -- framed for a murder he didn't commit. For others, he was a troublemaker, a violent revolutionary, and a dangerous man. But there was one fact on which everyone who knew him, from his most fervent supporters to his bitterest enemies, could agree. Tom Mooney was a real pain in the ass.

The son of an Irish immigrant coal miner and labor organizer, Mooney joined the Iron Molders Union at age 14. Mooney, a man large in stature and personality, became editor of the journal "Revolt" in 1911 and earned a reputation as a militant writer and speaker. He became friends with radical luminaries such as "Big Bill" Haywood and Mary "Mother" Jones. But there was a less attractive side to Mooney. He was belligerent and intolerant of others, even those who shared his political views. Still, his dynamism attracted followers. One was Rena Hermann, a young socialist and music teacher he married in 1911. Another was Warren Billings, a slight, boyish- looking man who became Mooney's assistant.

Mooney and Billings believed in direct action and worked with a radical wing of the International Brotherhood of Electrical Workers to sabotage PG&E transmission lines. Billings was offered $25 to deliver a suitcase to Sacramento. When he arrived, he went to the Silver Cup Saloon and waited for his contact to arrive. Detectives, who had been tipped off, seized the dynamite-filled suitcase and arrested Billings. Mooney was supposed to pick up the suitcase but was delayed in traffic and escaped. Billings was convicted of possession of explosives and sent to prison.

There were those on the other side who also believed in direct action, especially Martin Swenson, a ruthless Pinkerton detective, who worked for both PG&E and the railroads. In June 1916, after three PG&E utility towers were damaged by dynamite, Swenson approached Israel Weinberg, a cab driver who often drove Mooney, and offered him $5,000 to testify against him. "It wouldn't take much to convict Mooney," said Swenson. "Just a little circumstantial evidence. It wouldn't be necessary for you to say you remembered all the details." Weinberg turned him down.

But it wasn't only large corporations that hated Mooney. With his radical calls for industrial unionism, Mooney had become a thorn in the side of the San Francisco Labor Council, which represented the more moderate trade unions of the American Federation of Labor.

Then came the parade. It was the middle of World War I, and the drumbeats for America's entry on the Allied side were growing louder. Large corporations and manufacturers were sponsoring "Preparedness Day parades" around the country, and participation in these parades was considered a test of patriotism.

One of the largest parades, sponsored by the Chamber of Commerce, was to be in San Francisco on July 22. For weeks in advance, the Hearst newspapers enthusiastically covered preparations and quoted parade supporters, such as Defense League chairman Charles Hanlon, who proclaimed, "Every red-blooded American in San Francisco is aroused."

Opposing the parade were organized labor, religious leaders, and some of San Francisco's most reform-minded citizens. Radicals and anarchists also targeted the parade. An unsigned leaflet warned: "We are going to use a little direct action on the 22nd to show that militarism can't be forced on us and our children without a violent protest."

Mooney had been tipped off to these threats and pushed resolutions through his union warning that provocateurs might attempt to blacken the labor movement by causing a disturbance at the parade.

The San Francisco Preparedness Day parade was to be the largest ever held in the city.

The three-and-a-half-hour procession had 51,329 marchers, including 2,134 organizations, and 52 bands. The parade began at Steuart and Market streets at 1.30 p.m., led by Mayor "Sunny Jim" Rolph. Ten minutes later, a short, dark- complexioned man set a large tan suitcase down by the wall of the Ferry Exchange Saloon on the corner of Market Street and walked away.

At 2:06 p.m. all hell broke loose.

The time bomb inside the suitcase exploded, shooting hundreds of pieces of shrapnel into the street at three thousand feet per second. Ten people were killed and forty wounded. The steel pipe bomb was filled with metal slugs to make it more deadly. It was, and still is, the worst terrorist act in San Francisco history.

Police Lieutenant Duncan Matheson began evacuating the wounded and left another officer in charge at the scene. When he returned an hour later, he found the officer spraying the street with a fire hose, washing vital evidence down the sewer.

A $17,000 reward ($400,000 in today's money) was offered. The editor of the New York Times correctly predicted that a reward of that size would be "a sweepstake for perjurers."

Police had no real clues, so the newly formed bomb squad drew up a list of obvious suspects. Famous anarchists Alexander Berkman and Emma Goldman led the list, but left-wing labor activists Tom Mooney and Warren Billings also appeared as possible suspects. By Wednesday, July 26, the bomb squad had still not identified a suspect. But San Francisco DA Charles Frickert didn't care; he had already chosen the guilty parties. The last thing Frickert wanted was an honest investigation.

Three days earlier, on the night of the bombing, Martin Swenson, a Pinkerton detective working United Railroads, San Francisco's streetcar company, and PG&E, met privately with Frickert and told him that Mooney and Billings were the bombers. Swenson, who was to Mooney as Inspector Javert was to Jean Valjean, had been trying for months to frame Mooney for a previous PG&E bombing. Frickert, who had been elected with a secret $100,000 fund from United Railroads, agreed and put Swenson in charge of the investigation.

Their first step was to alter the facts to fit Mooney and Billings. To make the conspiracy more impressive, Tom's wife, Rena, labor organizer Edward Nolan, and cab driver Israel Weinberg were added as co-defendants.

Adjusting the description of the bombers was the first order of business. A number of witnesses had said the bombers were short, swarthy men, a description which fit neither Billings nor Mooney. One of the witnesses, John MacDonald, was approached and convinced to identify Mooney and Billings in exchange for a large share of the reward money. Other witnesses were induced to change their stories to fit the new narrative.

Frickert planned three trials as a kind of banquet of injustice. Billings, in the first trial, would serve as the appetizer. Mooney was the main course. For dessert, Frickert intended to send Rena, Nolan, and Weinberg to prison. Using perjured testimony and a stacked deck of prosecution-friendly jurors, Billings was convicted.

Frank Oxman, a cattle rancher, was the star witness at Mooney's trial. He claimed that he saw Tom and Rena Mooney, Billings, and Weinberg together in a car and then saw them deposit the suitcase on the curb. During cross-examination, he produced a sheet of paper on which he had written the license plate of Weinberg's car. Although the defense produced a photograph showing that Mooney was nowhere near the site of the bombing when the explosion occurred, Oxman's testimony convinced the jury, and Mooney was convicted. On February 24,1917, Mooney was sentenced to hang.

Just weeks later, Fremont Older, managing editor of the San Francisco Bulletin, received a bombshell, a series of letters Frank Oxman had written to a friend. In them, Oxman asked his friend to perjure himself for the reward money and admitted that he had not even been in San Francisco at the time of the bombing.

Older, San Francisco's pre-eminent journalist for over 40 years, made the Mooney case his personal crusade. For weeks, the Bulletin ran stories exposing the evidence that Frickert had manufactured against Mooney and Billings. Rena Mooney and her co-defendants were quickly acquitted in their trial, but Mooney and Billings were not able to get a new trial, and Mooney's execution date of May 17 was looming closer. Huge protest demonstrations were held around the world. The stench of the frame-up reached Washington where Woodrow Wilson, afraid of the effect that the case would have internationally, convinced the governor of California to commute Mooney's sentence.

Despite the evidence of their innocence, Mooney and Billings remained in San Quentin. The Mooney case became a great international cause célèbre for the next 23 years. "Free Tom Mooney!" screamed the banners in Moscow, New York, London, and Paris. It was often referred to as the American Dreyfus Case.

Culbert Olson was elected governor in 1939, the first Democrat to hold that office since the late 19th Century. He promptly pardoned Mooney, and the freed labor activist paraded down Market Street in triumph. That was Mooney's last hurrah. He was out of touch with the labor movement, and his attempt to divorce his loyal wife, Rena, cost him a good deal of support. His health, weakened by his years in jail, worsened, and by the time he died, in 1942, he was a forgotten man.

Warren Billings' life had a different ending. In 1936, young Josephine Rudolph was about to write a letter to Tom Mooney. "Everyone writes to Mooney," said her mother, "why don't you write to Warren Billings? Thus began a correspondence that led to romance; Josephine and Warren were married in 1940, the year he was released.

Warren, who had learned watchmaking in prison, opened a small shop on Market Street. Though he had every right to be bitter, he became a generous and forgiving man. He stayed active politically, demonstrated against McCarthy and the Vietnam War and lived happily with Josephine for the next thirty-two years. He died on September 5, 1972, beloved by all who knew him.

The Preparedness Day bombing has never been solved. The most likely candidates were two followers of radical anarchist Luigi Galleani, who believed in direct violent action.

One suspect was Celsten Eklund, a well- known San Francisco radical, mortally wounded by police in 1927 as he attempted to blow up Saints Peter and Paul Catholic church in San Francisco's North Beach. The other was Mario Buda, a bomb maker of deadly repute who constructed explosives filled with shrapnel in order to maximize casualties.

Buda was associated with Nicola Sacco and Bartolomeo Vanzetti, Italian anarchists whose conviction and execution for murder became the most famous and controversial case of the 1920s.

Buda is believed to have been responsible for the deadly 1920 Wall Street bombing, which was set in protest of the arrest of Sacco and Vanzetti. The Wall Street bombing killed 38 people and wounded hundreds. After the bombing, Buda fled to Italy where he spent five years in prison for his political activities. He worked as a shoemaker after his release until his death in 1963 at the age of 78.

Paul Drexler

The Zodiac Killer

SFPD wanted poster (SFPD, 1969)

It should be a rule that anyone who writes about the Zodiac killer must come up with a new suspect. The Zodiac's identity is the most famous unsolved murder mystery of modern times. No case has inspired as many theories and wild speculation and spread as much terror in California.

The case contains all the elements of a best-selling detective thriller: A series of random killings occurs. The killer sends threatening and bizarre letters to the newspapers. The letters contain mysterious ciphers, which may identify the killer. The City is crippled with fear, and the police are helpless. All that is needed is a

Kay Scarpetta, a Nero Wolfe or a Hercule Poirot to find the clues, break the code and solve the case. But real life is different. There was no magic detective, and the killer is still at large. Between 1968 and 1971, Zodiac killed at least five people in California.

The Crimes

The killings began on the evening of December 20, 1968, when Betty Lou Jensen and David Faraday, two Vallejo teenagers, were shot to death in a lovers' lane in Solano County, about an hour northeast of San Francisco. The investigation continued into the summer of 1969 but produced no viable suspects.

More than seven months after the murders of Jensen and Faraday, Darlene Ferrin and Michael Mageau were sitting in a car in Blue Rock Springs Park in Vallejo on the night of July 4, 1969. A car pulled up behind them. The driver stepped out holding a bright pencil-thin flashlight. At first, the couple thought it was a policeman, checking out the lovers' lane. But then the man pulled out a gun, walked to the passenger side and started firing. The fusillade killed Darlene and severely wounded Michael. The killer drove away and used a pay phone to call the Vallejo Police Department. When police dispatcher Nancy Slover answered, the caller said: "I want to report a murder. If you will go one mile east on Columbus Parkway, you will find kids in a brown car. They were shot with a nine- millimeter Luger. I also killed those kids last year. Goodbye."

Four weeks later, the San Francisco Chronicle, San Francisco Examiner and Vallejo Times Herald received letters from the killer containing details of the murder, along with a cipher that the writer claimed contained clues to his identity. A crossed-circle symbol had been drawn at the bottom of the page.

The letter writer threatened to go on a killing spree if the newspapers didn't print his letters. The newspapers complied and published the cipher and the letters.

Expert and amateur cryptographers raced to decode the cipher. While Navy and FBI cryptographers struggled, two amateurs, schoolteacher Donald Harden and his wife Bettye broke the code. The decoded cipher read:

> *"I like killing people because it is so much fun it is more fun than killing wild game in the forest because man is the most dangerous animal of all to kill something gives me the most thrilling experience it is even better than getting your rocks off with a girl the best part of it is that when I die I will be reborn in paradise and all the (people) I have killed will become my slaves I will not give you my name because you will try to slow down or stop my collecting of slaves for my afterlife. EBEORIETEMETHHPITI."*

The last 18 characters were supposed to reveal the Zodiac's real name if correctly deciphered.

Zodiac made numerous references to "The Most Dangerous Game," Richard Connell's famous short story about a deranged big game hunter who believes that hunting people is more challenging than hunting animals.

The cipher and its solution established two elements that were to make this case unique and unforgettable. The first element was a classic villain. The Zodiac was arrogant and egotistical, but he was clever. We hated and feared him. We could not wait for him to get his comeuppance.

The second element was the rise of the amateur sleuth. The assassination of the Kennedys and Martin Luther King just a few years before had changed the zeitgeist. The trust in authority had been cracked. Conspiracy theories had gone mainstream. The authorities and the professionals, ridiculed by Zodiac, seemed lost, nowhere near a solution. A schoolteacher and his wife, for God's sake, had humbled the mighty FBI. Thousands of people became obsessed with the case.

Then the case got even weirder.

On the afternoon of September 27, 1969, college students Bryan Hartnell and Cecelia Shepard had settled along the shore of Lake Berryessa when a man appeared wearing a bizarre, hooded costume that had a white crossed- circle stitched onto the front. The stranger held them at gunpoint while he bound them with a clothesline. He said he was an escaped prisoner who was trying to steal some money to get out of town. Then, when it seemed he was about to leave, he suddenly pulled out a foot-long knife and stabbed them repeatedly. He then walked over to Hartnell's car, drew a zodiac symbol on the door, the dates of his two shootings and "Sept 27 69 6:30 by knife." Shepard died from multiple stab wounds, Hartnell survived.

The Zodiac next brought his deadly act to San Francisco. On October 11, 1969, a man entered a cab driven by Paul Stine in Union Square in San Francisco and requested to be taken to an address in Presidio Heights. When the car stopped on Cherry and Washington streets, the man shot Stine once in the head and left the car. Three young men saw the crime and called the police. They described the killer as a white man, "5'8" tall, heavy build, reddish-blond crew cut hair, wearing eyeglasses, dark brown trousers, dark (navy blue or black) Parka jacket, dark shoes."

Two SFPD Officers were responding to the police call when they passed a white male adult who matched the description and was walking away from the area of the crime scene. They reportedly did not stop to question the man they observed that night due to a mistake in the police broadcast which described the suspect as a black male adult. Unconscious racism may have saved the Zodiac killer.

Two days later, a bloody piece of Paul Stine's shirt arrived at the Chronicle along with a threat to shoot at children on school buses. Patrol cars and aircraft followed buses to and from schools, and armed officers rode on board for added protection.

Between 1969 and 1974, the Zodiac killer sent 15 letters and four ciphers to newspapers and police. His letters would usually begin, "This is the Zodiac speaking" and would alternate between descriptions of his cleverness, taunts at the authorities, references to explosives and future crimes, and occasional ciphers.

He threatened to "do my thing" if his letters weren't published on the first page of the newspapers. The newspapers were happy to comply, knowing that the Zodiac was a huge circulation booster.

The first cipher was solved but contained no clue to the Zodiac's identity. The other three ciphers remain unsolved. Adding to the glamour of the case was Dave Toschi, the SFPD homicide inspector assigned to the investigation. Toschi was a detective whose flamboyant outfits and larger than life persona were the models for both Clint Eastwood's Dirty Harry Callahan and Steve McQueen's *Bullitt* characters.

Although police investigated more than 2,500 people, no Zodiac suspect was ever arrested. The identity of the Zodiac killer continues to fascinate people, and more than 50 websites are devoted to this case. Millions of people use these websites each month. A search for "Zodiac killer" on YouTube brings up 233,000 hits; the same search on Google yields more than 17 million hits. Tens of thousands of people, known as Zodiologists, have been working to find a solution.

In Blind Men and the Elephant, poet John Godfrey Saxe describes how six blind men of Indostan examine different parts of an elephant and come to completely different conclusions. He ends the poem with these stanzas:

*And so these men of Indostan,
disputed loud and long, each in his
own opinion, exceeding stiff and
strong, Though each was partly in the
right, all were in the wrong!*

Paul Drexler

> *So, oft in theologic wars, the*
> *disputants, I ween, tread on in utter*
> *ignorance, of what each other mean,*
> *and prate about the elephant, not one*
> *of them has seen!*

The parable of the blind men and the elephant is a good lens though which to view Zodiology. Zodiologists often have selective vision. They see evidence that links their suspect to the Zodiac but evidence to the contrary is invisible to them.

Evidence itself can be a slippery slope. Like love and promises, evidence can be elusive, delusionary, and complex. DNA is sometimes incomplete, fingerprints can be partial, handwriting analysis is subjective, and eyewitnesses are often unreliable. Seventy-five percent of people who were freed by DNA evidence had been convicted on the basis of eyewitness testimony. For example, although most people can estimate a person's height within four inches, they tend to underestimate the size of tall and large people.

The field of Zodiology became established with Robert Graysmith's bestselling book "Zodiac" in 1986. Graysmith, who worked at the SF Chronicle as a cartoonist during Zodiac's crime spree, developed an obsession with the case. For thirteen years, he attempted to decode the ciphers, amassing file cabinets full of information, and losing his marriage in the process. Graysmith's book became the basis of the 2007 movie Zodiac, a film, that, like its source, does not let the facts of the case get in the way of a good story. Zodiology reminds me of a religion where different sects compete to be the voice of truth. Robert

Graysmith was the first prophet of Zodiology, and it was Graysmith who identified the first, and for many, the best suspect for the Zodiac, Arthur Leigh Allen.

Since that time, the Zodiac case has become a thriving cottage industry, and, like any business, new products, e.g. suspects, must be introduced to meet the demands of true crime consumers. What follows is a selection of some of the more prominent suspects.

The Suspects

Arthur Leigh Allen

Arthur Leigh Allen, a convicted child molester who lived in Vallejo, has been the prime candidate for the Zodiac for decades. Allen was an early subject of the police investigation and was the most thoroughly investigated of all the 2,500 suspects. He was the subject of several search warrants over a 20-year period. He lived near one of the crime scenes and owned a Zodiac watch, which featured a zodiac sign that matched the letters. According to a former friend named Don Cheny, Allen had a difficult relationship with his mother and hated women.

Allen admitted to owning guns and told investigators that he was camping around the time of the Lake Berryessa killing and had two bloody knives in his car from killing a chicken. The most serious accusations came from Cheny who said that Allen had referenced "The Most Dangerous Game of All," and had once talked about hunting people in lover's lane and sending notes from the Zodiac to police.

Allen's handwriting did not match the Zodiac, and his fingerprints did not match those found at the Stine killing. Allen's DNA was not consistent with the partial DNA profile taken from the stamps on the letters. Witnesses described the Zodiac as 5'8" with blond crewcut hair. Allen was a balding six-footer.

Supporters of Allen as the Zodiac point out that one of the Zodiac's surviving victims identified Allen as his attacker. What they don't tell you is that at the time of the attack, this same witness told police that he only saw a side view of his attacker and didn't get a good look at him. His identification of Arthur Leigh Allen was done years after the attack.

Over the years, Don Cheney embellished his story to the point that it lost credibility.

Arthur Leigh Allen died in 2002 from complications of diabetes.

Richard Gaikowski

Shortly after the publication of "Zodiac" in 1986, Blaine -- an unemployed man living in a van -- named yet another man as a suspect. Blaine, who was also known as Purple Blaine and Goldcatcher, accused Richard Gaikowski, a former colleague at "Good Times," a 1960s underground newspaper, of being the Zodiac. Tom Voight, owner of zodiackiller.com, one of the most popular Zodiac websites, believed Blaine's story, even though there was no physical evidence linking Gaikowski to the Zodiac.

A key piece of evidence against Gaikowski came from a police operator who heard Zodiac speak for about 15 seconds. Ten years later, this operator identified Gaikowski's voice as that of the Zodiac. Really? Other than Louis Armstrong, how many voices could you positively identify ten years after a brief conversation?

Larry Kane

Larry Kane has been rumored to be linked to the disappearance of Donna Lass and the kidnapping of Kathleen Johns, two crimes that some people attribute to Zodiac. He was identified as bearing a strong likeness by the policeman who saw Zodiac shortly after the Paul Stine shooting. Kane was in a serious car accident in 1962 that damaged the left frontal lobe of his brain. This often leads to increased risk taking and destructive behavior. Brain scans of psychopaths have found low functioning in their left frontal lobe. Kane was arrested for burglary, theft, and peering in other people's windows. But there is no reliable evidence linking Kane to the Zodiac crimes, and his finger print did not match the print on Paul Stine's car.

The Serial Killers

Some Zodiologists have taken a shortcut by trying to make existing serial killers, such as Ted Kaczynski – known as the Unabomber -- and Manson family member, Bruce Davis, into the Zodiac. Both men have been cleared by authorities. Kaczynski was not living in the Bay Area during the Zodiac period. As for Bruce Davis, when was the last time you saw a Manson family member with a crew cut?

The most imaginative serial killer theory is that of John Cameron, a former Montana detective, who claims that Ed Edwards, a convicted killer of five, is the Zodiac. According to Cameron, Edwards also killed Jimmy Hoffa, the Black Dahlia, JonBenet Ramsey, and the twenty-seven children in Atlanta. Despite this assault on reality (or perhaps because of it) Cameron got a six-part TV series, "He Did it," from Paramount to explore his delusions.

My Father Was the Zodiac!

Guy Ward Hendrickson

Deborah Perez made headlines when she claimed that her father, Guy Ward Hendrickson, was the Zodiac. Of course, she also claimed that she was the daughter of John F. Kennedy.

George Hill Hodel

Hodel was accused by his son, former LA homicide detective Steve Hodel. Of all the possible suspects, Dr. George Hodel is the most like Dr. Hannibal Lecter, the Picasso of fictional serial killers. Hodel was a brilliant student, a musical prodigy, a writer and a doctor. He was a charming, cosmopolitan man, friends with film director John Huston, and surrealist artists Man Ray and Marcel Duchamp.

But Hodel had a dark side. He was an abortionist, involved with police corruption, and was accused by his daughter of sexual abuse. He was also a major suspect in the 1947 Black Dahlia killing, LAs most iconic unsolved killing.

There are just a few problems with Dr. George Hodel being the Zodiac. He was the wrong age, wrong body type and had the wrong face. George Hodel was 58 years old at the time of the Zodiac killings: He was slender and always wore a mustache.

Earl Van Best

The latest member of the "Daddy did it" school of Zodiologists is Gary Stewart, who claims his father, Earl Van Best, was the Zodiac. Because Stewart's book "The Most Dangerous Animal of All," was published by a major publisher (Harper Collins) it received more publicity and was given more credibility than others. With the exception of Van Best's resemblance to the composite sketch of the Zodiac and a police record, the evidence is thin.

Stewart's key piece of evidence is a handwriting expert's conclusion that Van Best's handwriting is that of the Zodiac. The handwriting expert was so proud of himself that he wrote his own book on solving the Zodiac case. The main handwriting sample was Van Best's writing on his marriage certificate. Recent research, however, showed that the writing on the wedding certificate was done not by Van Best, but by the minister. So, either the handwriting expert is wrong, or a Methodist minister in Reno, Nevada, is the Zodiac.

This is the Zodiac speaking

I have become very upset with
the people of San Fran Bay
Area. They have **not** complied
with my wishes for them to
wear some nice ⊕ buttons.
I promiced to punish them
if they didnot comply, by
anilating a full School Bass.
But now school is out for
the summer, so I panished
them in an another way.
I shot a man sitting in
a parked car with a .38.

⊕-12   SFPD-0

The Map coupled with this
code will tell you whore the
bomb is set. You have antill
next Fall to dig it up. ⊕

C Δ J I ■ O ⏧ ⊥ A M ⏞ ▲ Ω O R T G
X ⊙ F D V ꝡ ▣ H C Ɛ L ⊕ P W Δ

*For weeks before this note, police accompanied
school buses in San Francisco.*

NONDENOMINATIONAL ZODIOLOGY

Zodiologists.com is a website that believes none of the current suspects are the Zodiac Killer. They put a strong emphasis on decoding the Zodiac ciphers and are developing a new Zodiac Killer profile that is "based on scientific method and deductive reasoning."

Zodiac Atheists

In "The Myth of the Zodiac Killer," Thomas Horan claims that Zodiac committed none of the murders. He believes the Zodiac character was a literary hoax designed to sell more papers. Horan claims the piece of Stine's shirt that was received by the Chronicle had been stolen from the morgue, presumably by a rogue reporter.

The Zodiac killings occurred almost 50 years ago, yet interest remains high. Each year, new suspects are revealed and debunked. On crime anniversaries, hundreds of Zodiologists descend on the murder site for meetings that are part crime seminar, part high school reunion.

The Zodiac claimed to have killed 37 victims. Authorities believe this number is greatly exaggerated, but there are a few additional crimes in which the Zodiac is suspected.

I asked Michael Butterfield (*zodiackillerfacts.com*), one of the more level-headed Zodiologists, for someone he considers a possible Zodiac suspect, and he mentioned Ross Sullivan, a suspect in a 1966 murder case in Riverside, California.

Cheryl Bates, a college student, was beaten and stabbed to death in the Southern California city. Bates had been studying in the college library prior to the attack. Her car was found intentionally disabled approximately 100 yards from the alley. Taunting letters were sent to the police and the victim's father. Confessions were mailed to the Riverside Police Department and the Riverside Press-Enterprise newspaper. A poem relating to the murder was carved into a desk at the Riverside City College library. Riverside police noted similarities between this case and the Zodiac in 1969. A state handwriting expert linked the poem to the Zodiac

In 1971, Zodiac sent a letter to the Los Angeles Times accepting responsibility for the Bates crime. Ross Sullivan worked at the Riverside City College library, near where Bates's body was found. He was a large, strange man who frightened his coworkers. Sullivan wore an Army jacket and military-style boots like those that left footprints at the Lake Berryessa stabbings. Sullivan disappeared for several days after the Bates murder, and when he returned, he was wearing completely different clothes. Sullivan had a crew cut and wore glasses similar to the composite sketch of the Zodiac. Sullivan moved to Northern California in 1967 and was hospitalized several times for bipolar disorder and schizophrenia. He studied cryptology in college and his handwriting has similarities to Zodiac's.

There is no evidence placing him near any of the Zodiac killings, and at 6'3" and 260 pounds, he was substantially larger than descriptions of Zodiac. He reportedly died of heart failure in 1977 in Santa Cruz, California.

As the Zodiac case passes its golden anniversary, it enters the pantheon of legendary mysteries, joining Jack the Ripper, the Kennedy assassination and others. Each year or so, a new suspect will emerge, a new book written, another true crime network will feature a "new investigation" of the Zodiac. Who knows what the future will bring? Maybe Zodiac really is Ted Cruz.

Paul Drexler

The Radian Theory

In June 1970, Zodiac sent a letter containing a map of the San Francisco Bay Area. The letter included a cipher along with the explanation that the map and the code would lead authorities to a buried bomb. The letter contains a mathematical term, "radian" (an angle valued between 57 and 58 degrees) in the instructions.

In 1980, Gareth Penn drew a radian angle on a map of the Bay Area. By placing the top of the angle on Mt. Diablo and rotating the radian, he found that one leg of the radian passed through the site of the Blue Rock Springs murder and the other passed through the site of the Presidio Heights murder scene. 'It was the most shocking experience of my entire life," Penn wrote.

Penn, who held two master's degrees from U.C. Berkeley and a Fulbright Scholarship added an intellectual patina to Zodiology. He worked as a research librarian and wrote occasional articles for the local Mensa journal. Penn concluded that the Zodiac murders were geographical in nature and part of a message that could be seen from the perspective of a map or an airplane.

Penn theorized that the murders were a sinister variant of environmental art or earthworks, an art movement that emerged in the 1960s and 1970s. The Zodiac doesn't know his victims. What's important to him is not who his victims are, but where they are. The Zodiac is a brilliant mad artist whose canvas is the earth, whose victims are the sculptural elements, and whose chisels are knives and guns.

Penn also noticed a unifying theme in the murder locations -- Lake Herman Road, Blue Rock Springs, Lake Berryessa. The locations all referred to water. Penn's Radian theory was embraced by many Zodiologists as a brilliant insight and has become part of the Zodiology mythos. But Gareth Penn was just getting started.

Penn combined the water theme with the Radian theory and began trying to identify them. He searched the biographical artist directory in the local Napa County library in search of a sculptor whose name was related to water, looking specifically for an artist whose initials were HOH, the chemical formula for water (H_2O).

He found a sculptor cross-referenced under the name O'Hare, but the sculptor was a 73-year- old woman. She had a son, however, named Michael Henry O'Hare. "It wasn't perfect," Penn admitted. "He wasn't the sculptor, but the sculptor's son. And he wasn't an HOH but an MHOH. Even so, the hairs on my arm were standing on end."

By the mid-1980s, Penn was convinced that he had solved the case, and in 1987, he revealed his discovery to the world with his self-published book, "Times-17." The book began with a discourse on the etymology of language, whisking the reader through Genesis, Dante, the Kabballah, Galileo, Samuel Morse, and George Boole. Then, having established his intellectual credentials, Penn began his display of acrobatic logic.

Penn's logic was like a mountain goat, jumping from improbable assumption to dubious deduction in search of an incredible conclusion. Using a combination of Kabbalah and Morse code, Penn declared that he had stumbled onto Zodiac's private language ("Zodiacese"). Penn deduced that the number "38" has great significance in Zodiacese. He knew that Michael O'Hare had been on the Harvard Rifle Team and was the editor of a student literary periodical titled Cambridge 38. Penn's numerological analysis also revealed other suspicious ties between O'Hare, the number 17, and the Zodiac.

Then Penn made his Icarus-like flight into the sun of logic and crashed. Using selective numerology, invented connections and quasi- intellectual logic, Penn declared that Michael O'Hare, then a brilliant young Harvard Public Policy lecturer, was the Zodiac.

Penn also accused O'Hare of the murder of Harvard graduate student Joan Webster in Boston, which expanded his deadly canvas to three thousand miles. Penn made little headway with his crusade, other than confounding Michael O'Hare. O'Hare, whose academic career continued to rise, decided that ignoring Penn was the best strategy.

In 1990, in a bit of karmic payback, Gareth Penn himself was accused of being a member of the Zodiac team. Ray Grant, another Mensa member, believed in Penn's Radian theory but took it a step further. According to Grant, there were four people involved in the Zodiac murders. They were the trigger man, Michael O'Hare; the press agent, Gareth Penn; the cryptographer, Gareth's father Hugh Penn; and the artistic mastermind, O'Hare's mother, Berta Margulies. Grant predicted that the Zodiac conspiracy would lead to a "Terminus Event," a horrific crime in which a skyscraper in Cambridge would be blown to bits in the year 2000. He now takes credit for preventing this catastrophe.

I used to be surprised when people believed these far-fetched theories. But in this new post-fact, alternative reality, where Hillary Clinton sells children out of a pizza parlor and the twenty children killed at Sandy Hook were really method actors, any theory, if yelled with enough conviction, can attract millions of true believers. I can almost hear Alex Jones saying: "The globalists have been hiding the truth about the Zodiac conspiracy for almost fifty years, but we know the real facts. We know Zodiac has been hiding in plain sight, on the walls and cubicles of unsuspecting America. He is heavy set, with light, short, curly hair, with horn-rimmed glasses. We know he works as a shill for the corporate media, knows how to write code and has trouble with women. What the deep state doesn't want you to know... is that

The Zodiac   **Is Dilbert**

Paul Drexler

BONUS CASE:

Killer Confectioner: The Sweet Gifts of Cordelia Botkin

Chocolate has been an integral part of San Francisco since the Gold Rush. The two oldest chocolate companies in the U.S. -- Ghirardelli and Guittard -- both started in San Francisco in the early 1850's. This tradition continues today with artisanal chocolate makers, such as TCHO and Dandelion making small batches of chocolate. But there was one 19th century chocolatier, Cordelia Botkin, who is never mentioned.

Therin lies a story

It all started in Golden Gate Park in September 1895 where John Dunning an Associated Press Manager, met Cordelia Botkin. They struck up an immediate friendship based on a shared perception; their spouses did not understand them. Dunning had a wife and young daughter in San Francisco – she was religious- Cordelia had a grown son and was separated and living .

During the next two years Dunning and Botkin carried on an affair at her apartment at 927 Geary Street. Adultery seemed to be a gateway vice for

Dunning; he started drinking heavily, and betting unsuccessfully at the racetrack. His gambling necessitated a fourth vice, embezzling money from the Associated Press, which led to his firing.

As a result, his wife Mary and his daughter moved back to Dover, Maryland to live with her father, John Pennington, a former congressman.

John moved into a room at 927 Geary where he became part of an unusual relationship with Cordelia, her son Beverly and his mistress, a widow named Louise Seely.

They went to the track together and often had loud boozy parties, financed by Cordelia's generous monthly allowance from her husband, a man with the unlikely name of Welcome Botkin.

Soon, Dunning's wife Mary began receiving anonymous letters from "a friend" telling her that her husband had been keeping company with " an attractive woman" and warning her not to reconcile with her husband. Mary turned the letters over to her father for safekeeping.

By 1898 Dunning's ardor for Cordelia had cooled considerably. "She is jolly company but has raised merry hell several times. She wants me all to herself and gets jealous if I look at another woman," he later testified. The Spanish American War gave Dunning his chance to escape. He was rehired as the AP's top reporter in the conflict and sent to Puerto Rico.

Before he left, Dunning told Cordelia that he had reconciled with his wife and would not be returning to San Francisco. Cordelia begged him not to go and tried to get an appointment as a nurse in the conflict to no avail.

A few months later, on August 9, 1898 Mary Dunning received a package of candy and handkerchief with note saying "with love to yourself and your baby. -- Mrs. C. "

Mary was having a family dinner with her parents, her sister-in-law, Mrs. Deane and other assorted friends and children. After dinner she passed around the chocolates. That evening everyone who ate the candies were stricken with stomach pains and vomiting. Most of them recovered, but Mary and Mrs. Deane, who had consumed the most, both died within two days.

Mr. Pennington had the candies examined by Dr Bishop and they were found to be loaded with arsenic. Pennington also noticed the similarity between the handwriting on the package and the handwriting on the anonymous notes. John Dunning was summoned, and he immediately recognized the handwriting on the notes as Cordelia's. Botkin denied authorship of the notes and said that an unnamed enemy (presumably Louise Seeley, her son's mistress) was responsible but evidence against her was growing.

But first there was a battle between California, where the crime began, and Maryland, where the crime occurred, to see who had jurisdiction to try the case. A judge ruled that Cordelia could not be extradited to place where she had never been, so California got the case.

Although SFPD Police Chief Isaiah Lees led the investigation both The San Francisco Chronicle and the Examiner competed fiercely each trying to be the first to find evidence of Cordelia's guilt. She was soon arrested and brought to trial. Her trial was standing room only and hundreds of people waited outside the courtroom. For their benefit the *Examiner* erected a public bulletin board, where it posted up-to-the-minute reports of the trial's progress. John Dunning testified that Cordelia knew that his wife loved sweets and had a friend named Mrs. Corbally in San Francisco. A handwriting expert testified that Cordelia had written the note accompanying the poisoned chocolates. Witnesses also identified Cordelia as the person who bought the chocolates and the arsenic.

Described by an Examiner reporter as "a smug, self satisfied cunning little woman, as full of funny little affectations as a porcupine of quills," Cordelia denied all charges.

After four hours of deliberation the jury found Cordelia guilty. Judge Carroll Cook sentenced Cordelia to life in prison. Cordelia's chocolates seemed to catch the public's imagination and at least two women sent poisoned candy to themselves to gain their 15 minutes of fame.

Cordelia's actions seemed to put a curse on her family. her lover , mother, sister, and son and former husband all died soon after her conviction.

Cordelia was lodged in the city jail while her case was appealed but she continued to make the news. In 1900 Judge Cook was riding on the Guerrero streetcar when he noticed, with shock that Cordelia was sitting eight rows away from him, on the same car. Though it appeared that Cordelia had been trading favors for freedom with the prison guards, jail officials denied the charges and claimed that Judge Cook had mistakenly identified a Cordelia look alike. Cordelia suggested that her doppelganger might have sent the poison.

In 1904 Cordelia was granted a new trial on a procedural error by the judge. Her new attorney George Knight launched a spirited defense in which he claimed that the women were killed by any or all of the following: Dr Bishop, ptomaine poisoning from rotten fish, and/or the candy company, through using unclean copper kettles.

The verdict was the same, Guilty!

In 1906 ,after the San Francisco earthquake, Botkin was sent to San Quentin where she died of "softening of the brain, due to melancholy" on March 7, 1910.

Postscript:

There is a heartwarming story from the Daily Press of Sheboygan Wisconsin, dated May 21, 1910 about Cordelia's burial, which took place in a small town in Northern California where her parents lived. According to this story there was a kind conspiracy in the town to keep the news of Cordelia's guilt from her parents. Though the local newspaper covered the case, it was always called "The Dunning Case." Cordelia was always referred to as "the accused" and her real name was never mentioned. Mrs. Botkin's father and mother never learned that Cordelia had died in prison.

"And all the little village took hold of hands and formed around the old people a cordon of silence, and woe to anyone who dared to try to break through. We are prone to think of heaven as a place far removed from everything we know here on this earth. But, oh that little village out there, nestling in the green, green hills of smiling California! I wonder if the angels do not look down upon it and smile."

It's a nice story, but untrue , Cordelia's mother died in 1900, shortly after Cordelia's conviction.

Appreciation

Enjoy this book? You can make a big difference.

Reviews are one of the most powerful tools when it comes to book ranking, exposure and future sales. I have a bunch of loyal readers, and honest reviews of my books help bring them to the attention of other readers.

If you've enjoyed this book, I would be very grateful if you'd take a few minutes to write a brief review on Amazon.

Thank you so much, Paul

Paul Drexler

About the Author

Paul Drexler has been writing about San Francisco crime since 1984. He worked for years with the late Kevin Mullen, a retired deputy chief of the San Francisco Police Department, developing *Crooks Tours of San Francisco*, which offers walking crime tours of Chinatown and the Barbary Coast.

Paul designed and co-produced *SFPD Homicide*, an interactive, award-winning, true-crime video game that has been used to teach police procedures.

His column, "*Notorious Crooks*," appeared regularly in the Sunday San Francisco Examiner from 2014 to 2018.

He has taught crime history at San Francisco State and appeared on the Discovery ID Network show, *Deadly Women*, as an expert on San Francisco murderesses and on *Spike TV* as an expert on the Zodiac Killer. In July 2017, Paul received the *Oscar Lewis Award* from the San Francisco History Association for his writing on San Francisco.

Contact Information

Crookstour website:

https://www.crookstour.com/

Twitter:

https://twitter.com/pdrexler1

Paul Drexler
30 Paloma Ave
San Francisco, Ca 94127

pdrexler8@gmail.com

SOURCES

The Unkindest Cut of All Buck Kelly
SF Chronicle Oct 22, 1926
Oakland Tribune July 26, 1927
San Mateo Times Dec 10, 1926
San Francisco Examiner Oct 20,22,25, Dec 22,
    1926,
Sept 12, 1927, May 12, 20, 1928
Petaluma Courier May 11,15, 1928
Oakland Tribune Tue, Oct 19, 1926 · Page 2
    Oakland Tribune Oct 21
Santa Cruz Evening News Tue, Oct 19, 1926 ·
    Page 1 Mullen, Kevin (2005) The Toughest
    Gang in Town Noir Publications

The Gorilla Killer Earle Nelson
Manitoba Tribune June 13, 16 1927
Phil. Inquirer Nov 14, 1925, May 1, 1927
LA Times Aug 12, 1926, Feb 2, April 20, April 21,
    1927 Salt Lake Telegram Dec 6,1926
Eugene Guard, Oregon Oct 28, 1926
Graysmith, Robert (2009) The Laughing Gorilla,
    Berkeley Books
San Francisco Examiner, Saturday, June 18, 1927
    - Page 7
NY Daily News July 14, 1929
The San Bernardino County Sun Wed, Aug 11,
    1926 · Page 2
The Daily Times Davenport, Iowa, Fri, Jan 07,
    1927 · Page 1
San Bernardino County Sun Fri, Jun 10, 1927 ·
    Page 3
The Buttermilk Bluebeard
San Francisco Examiner Dec 20, 1945 p. 6.

Minneapolis Star Tribune April 28, 1946 St. Louis Post-Dispatch Sun, Jan 06, 1946 Oakland Tribune Sun, Jul 9, 16, 23, 1950
Valley Morning Star Cameron, Texas, Sun, Dec 23, 1945 · Page 11

The Murderous Millionaire William Thoresen

Wall, Glenn (2013) Sympathy Vote: A Reinvestigation of the Valerie Percy Murder, Glenn Wall Publishing,
Louise Thoresen, E.M. Nathanson (1974) It Gave Everyone Something to Do, M. Evans and Co
"Sad Cinderella and her Gun Happy Millionaire", True Police Cases, Jan 1971
San Francisco Chronicle Jan 7, 1970
Daily Independent Journal Sat, Apr 22, 1967 · Page 26 Tucson Daily Citizen Mon, Dec 28, 1964 · Page 18

The Great Diamond Hoax Asbury Harpending

Harpending , Asbury The Great Diamond Hoax. 1916 San Francisco Chronicle Nov 26, Dec 12, 1872, Sept 5, 1915
San Francisco Bulletin December 6, 1872, August 25, 1874

Big Bertha Bertha Heyman

Byrnes, Thomas, Professional Criminals of America 1886
San Francisco Chronicle 11 Feb 1889, Mon • Page 1 The Los Angeles Times Sat, Nov 17, 1888 · Page 4
The San Francisco Call Sat, Jan 28, 1893 · Page 2 Los Angeles Herald Thu, Aug 07, 1890 · Page 5 The San Francisco Call Fri, Feb 05, 1892 · Page 7 The Los Angeles Times Tue, Jul 08, 1890 · Page 4

The Man of a 1000 Aliases Andrew John Gibson

New York Times September 2, 1897

San Francisco Call April 7, 1903 , Sat, Feb 17, 1912 The Sydney Morning Herald Fri, Oct 20, 1916 · Page 8, Fri, Mar 01, 1940 · Page 12

The Guardian, London, Tue, Jan 25, 1938 · Page 15 Oakland Tribune Sun, Feb 13, 1916 · Page 7

The Guardian London, 25 Jan 1938, Tue • Page 15 Oakland Tribune, 13 Feb 1916, Sun • Page 7

Great Crimes of the West, (1929) Pete Fanning

The Father of Electric Medicine Dr. Albert Abrams

Dr. Albert Abrams (1900) "Scattered Leaves from a Physician's Diary"

The San Francisco Call, Nov 20, 1912 pg. 3, Sun, Jul 13, 1913

San Francisco Chronicle Sat, Feb 19, May 8,1921, Jan 13, 1970

Van Vleck, Richard, "Electronic Reactions of Albert Abrams" From American Artifacts No.39

Jarvis, William T Ph.D. "Radionics and Albert Abrams, M.D" 1995

ALBERT ABRAMS, A.M., M.D., LL.D, F.R.M.S., Museum of Quackery
 http://www.museumofquackery.com/amquacks/abrams.htm

The History of Radionics Dr. Albert Abrams https://radionicsspectro.com/2016/02/13/the-history-of-radionics/

Queen of Grudges Isabella J. Martin

San Francisco Chronicle July 20, July 26, August 14, 1894, June 16, 1895, July 21, Dec 16, 1908, May 28, 1912

San Francisco Examiner Sat, Jul 08 1893, Page 12 Sun, Feb 23, 1908 · Page 23

The San Francisco Call Jun 25 1895, Tue • Page 14 AP "Baby John Said He Tried to Blow Up Dingee's Home" May 8, 1908

The Jazzmania Murderer Dorothy Ellingson
San Francisco Examiner Jan 15- 31 1926
Oakland Tribune March 6, 1933
San Francisco Chronicle March 28, 1926,
   November 15, 1927, March 6, 1932, August 21,
   1932, February 9, 1955

The Duchess: A Female Fagin Juanita Spinelli
San Francisco Examiner April 18, July 14, 1940,
   June 21, Nov 26, 1941
The Fresno Bee The Republican Jul 10, 1941 ·
   Page 2 Oakland Tribune Tue, Nov 25, 1941 ·
   Page 19
The Fresno Bee The Republican Thu, Jul 10, 1941 ·
   Page 2
Oakland Tribune July 10, Tue, Nov 25, 1941 ·
   Page 1
The Grandma From Hell Iva Kroeger
The Press Democrat
(Santa Rosa, California) Sun, Feb 27, 1966 Page
   2,
Mar 02 1987, Mon • Page 2
San Francisco Police Department Investigators
   notes, Nov 1, 1961 – Sept 1962
San Francisco Chronicle July 3, July 4, 1964,
   May 16, 1971
Confidential Detective Cases, "California's
   Incredible Iva Kroeger- Her Life, Her lies, Her
   Killings" March 1964
Official Detective Stories, "Solving the Crime That
   Rocked the West Coast" Dec 1962
True Detective, "California Corpses in Concrete"
   Jan 1963

Purveyors of Sin:
King of the Tenderloin Jerome Bassity

> *San Francisco Chronicle, January 22, 1898,*
> *October 5, 1905 September 13, 27,1907,*
> *February 13, 1908, July 13, 23, 1913, November*
> *30, 1922*

> *San Francisco Examiner April 28, 1910, May 1,*
> *1910, Aug 28, 1910, July 31, 1913, March 26,*
> *1916, Nov 10, 1920, Nov 6, 1922*

> *The San Francisco Call April 26,1901, Aug 18,*
> *1905 Asbury, Herbert The Barbary Coast, 1933*

A Necessary Evil Inez Burns

> *San Francisco Chronicle Nov 8, 1945, March 6,*
> *1946, Aug 25, 1948, March 27, 1956*

> *San Francisco Examiner May 6, 1938, October*
> *12, 1939, March 17, 1940, Oct 2, 1945, Jan 21-*
> *30, Sept 6, 1946, June 5, 1947, May 9, 1954, Aug*
> *25,1954*

> *Bloom, Stephen, The Audacity of Inez Burns,*
> *Regan Arts 2018*

San Francisco's Gambling Czar Elmer "Bones" Remmer

> *San Francisco Examiner, April 23,1948*
> *CASINO CHIP AND TOKEN NEWS | 2000 pg 87*
> *Reno Gazette-Journal, April 24, 1948*
> *Oakland Tribune Fri, Apr 30, 1948 · Page 21*
> *The Fresno Bee The Republican· Wed, Jun 12,*
> *1963 · Page 6*
> *Santa Cruz Sentinel Wed, Dec 12, 1951 · Page 2*
> *The Bakersfield Californian Wed, Nov 17, 1948 ·*
> *Page 1 The San Bernardino County Sun · Fri,*
> *Dec 14, 1951 · Page 10*

Paul Drexler

From Madam to Mayor

*San Francisco Chronicle September 25, 1940, Jan
5, 1944, Jan 12, 1944, Aug 23, 1962, February 2,
1982*

*San Francisco Examiner Aug 25, 1936, Sept 20,
1939 Bonagura, Marc "The Tiger is Dead", 1982*

*Gentry, Curt The Madams of San Francisco, 1962
Doubleday*

*Stanford, Sally The Lady of the House, 1966
Putnam*

A Study in Phrenology William Frederick

*The San Francisco Call, 29 Jun 1893, Thu • Page
2 The San Francisco Call, Sat, Mar 24, 1894 ·
Page 3 Herald Sat, Jul 27, 1895 · Page 1*

*Oakland Tribune, Fri, Jul 26, 1895 · Page 1 Pete
Fanning, Great Crimes of the West, 1929*

King of the Escape Artists Roy Gardner

San Bernardino Daily Sun Oct 13,1920

The Los Angeles Times Tue, Sept 06, 1921 ·

*The San Bernardino County Sun Sept 6, 1921, Fri,
Jan 12, 1940 ·*

*Oakland Tribune Sun, Dec 17, 1922 · Page 71,
Mon Nov 26, 1934*

*Santa Ana Register Thu, Mar 09, 1939 · Page 1
Gardner, Roy (1928) Hellcatraz,*

Manhunt
Joe Tanko and Floyd Hall

California State archives

*1926 Oakland Tribune Saturday, April 22, 25,
May 7, 1925 - Page 1 , Feb 16, 1956 · Page 3*

*San Francisco Examiner April 14, April 25, 1925,
Nov 14, 23,1926, March 17,1928*

*Daily Independent Journal San Rafael, Marin,
California Thu, Feb 16, 1956 · Page 1*

*The News-Review Roseburg, Douglas, Oregon
Sat, May 02, 1925 · Page 1*

The Yacht Bandits
Lloyd Sampsell and Ethan McNabb

Oakland Tribune Fri, Jun 13, 1930 · Page 3
Minneapolis Star Tribune Sun, May 1, 1932 ·
Page 53 The Weekly Pioneer-Times Deadwood,
South Dakota, Thu, Mar 26, 1908 · Page 7

The San Francisco Examiner Jul 13, 1922, Thu •
Page 15

Oakland Tribune, Thu, Feb 16, 1956 · Page 3
Oakland Tribune Fri, Jun 13, 1930 · Page 3 Tue,
Feb 28, 1933 · Page 16

San Francisco Chronicle, July 16 , 1950 p. 11 Don
Chaddock, Inside CDCR editor

The Los Angeles Times Thu, Jul 13, Jul 21, 1922

Men At Their Worst, Leo Stanley, D. Appleton
Century Company 1940

My Most Unforgettable Convicts, Leo Stanley,
Greyward Publishing 1967

Jack B. Olympius testimony, Volume III:
Witnesses Before the Governor's Committee on
Investigation of Folsom Prison, CSA, Earl
Warren Papers – Governor's Committee on
Penal Affairs – 1943-44.

On Investigation of Folsom Prison, pp. 921—929.
CSA, Earl Warren Papers – Governor's
Committee on Penal Affairs – 1943-44.
F3640:960.

61 McGraw to Plummer, March 2, 1943, from
San Quentin. Archived in Folsom Inmate Case
Files, Burroughs McGraw, 22230. F3745:519.

63 Lyle Egan, Volume IV: Witnesses Before the
Governor's Committee on Investigation of
Folsom Prison, p. 818. CSA, Earl Warren
Papers – Governor's Committee on Penal
Affairs – 1943-44. F3640:959.

68 Capt. William J. Ryan testimony, Volume II:
Witnesses Before the Governor's Committee on
Investigation of Folsom Prison, pp. 399-436,
esp. 428. California State Archives Earl

Warren Papers Department of Corrections
Records Board of Prison Directors Minutes
Governor's Committee on Penal Affairs
Institutions Department of Corrections
Records, F3717: 1937-1943, 1943-1944
Correspondence, 1852-
89, Records Relating to San Quentin Prison
Inmate Case Files, 1890-1958 Inmate Indexes,
1851-1940 Inmate Registers, 1940-1947
Identification Photograph Cards, 1907-1946
Records Relating to Folsom State Prison
Inmate Case Files, 1940-44 Inmate Registers,
1940-1949 Identification Photograph Cards,
1923-1945

Institutions

California State Archives Earl Warren Papers
Department of Corrections Records Board of
Prison Directors Minutes Governor's
Committee on Penal Affairs Institutions
Department of Corrections Records, F3717:
Folsom Minute Books, 1884,1937-1943 San
Quentin, Folsom Summary Books, 1943-1944
Correspondence, 1852-89, 1931-1944 Folsom
Minute Books, 1932,1943-1945 Records
Relating to San Quentin Prison Inmate Case
Files, 1890-1958 Inmate Indexes, 1851-1940
Inmate Registers, 1940-1947 Identification
Photograph Cards, 1907-1946 Records Relating
to Folsom State Prison Inmate Case Files, 1881-
1942 Numerical Inmate Register, 1940-44
Inmate Registers, 1940-1949 Identification
Photograph Cards, 1941-48,
San Quentin prison records for Lloyd Sampsell
Letters from Lloyd Sampsell to his son –
private collection

A Magical Murder Mystery Milton F. Andrews

San Francisco Chronicle
Los Angeles Herald, 20 August 1899
San Francisco Call Aug 16, 1899
*Whaley, Bert with Jeff Busby and Martin
  Gardner The Man Who Was Erdnase 1991*
*The Expert at the Card Table by S.W. Erdnase,
  1902 Conversations with Ricky Jay*
*The San Francisco Call Tue, Nov 07, 1905 · Page
  3 San Francisco Chronicle Tue, Nov 07, 1905 ·
  Page 1 Sun, Nov 12, 1905*

A Terrorist Whodunit Tom Mooney Warren Billings

*San Francisco Examiner July 29, 1916, June 1-10,
  1917, July 1-8, 1917, Nov 29, 1918, Dec 2, 1931 Jan
  8,1939*
*San Francisco Chronicle Feb 3, 1917, p. 3, Nov 19,
  1918*
*Gentry, Curt Frame-up: The Incredible Case of
  Tom Mooney and Warren Billings 1967*

The World of Zodiology

*Graysmith, Robert (1986) Zodiac: The Shocking
  True Story of the Hunt for the Nation's Most
  Elusive Serial Killer*
*Penn Gareth, Times-17. (1989) The Amazing
  Story of the Zodiac Murders in California and
  Massachusetts, Kelleher, Michael D. Ph.D. and
  David Van Nuys (2001) This Is the Zodiac
  Speaking: Into the Mind of a Serial Killer*
*Horan, Thomas Henry (2012) The Great Zodiac
  Killer Hoax of 1969*
*Stewart, Gary and Susan Mustafa, (2014) The
  Most Dangerous Animal of All: Searching for
  My Father . . . and Finding the Zodiac Killer*
Grant, Ray (2015) ZODIAC KILLER SOLVED
*Hodel, Steve (2015) Most Evil: Avenger, Zodiac,
  and the Further Serial Murders of Dr. George*

Hill Hodel Fraley, Craig (2015) Zodiac Killer Afterthoughts Sechrest, Michael D. and Tom Voigt (2017) Zodiac Code: Solved: Confession of the Zodiac Killer Cameron, John (2018) It's Me, Edward Wayne Edwards: the Serial Killer You Never Heard Of Zodiackiller.com Zodiackillerfacts.com Zodiackillerciphers.com Zodiacrevisited.com

Killer Confectioner: The Sweet Gifts of Cordelia Botkin

Duke, Thomas, Celebrated Criminal Cases of America, 1910

Mullen, Kevin, research notes

San Francisco Chronicle, July, August 1898, December 30, 1898

San Francisco Examiner, August 3, 1904, October 30, 1908

San Francisco Call, August 20, 1898

San Francisco Call, March 8, 1910

Made in the USA
Las Vegas, NV
06 September 2021

29679646R00118